BLOOD PRESSURE

The Essential Guide

Dr Justine
Davies

First published in Great Britain in 2010 by
Need2Know
Remus House
Coltsfoot Drive
Peterborough
PE2 9JX
Telephone 01733 898103
Fax 01733 313524
www.need2knowbooks.co.uk

Need2Know is an imprint of Forward Press Ltd.
www.forwardpress.co.uk
All Rights Reserved
© Justine Davies 2010
SB ISBN 978-1-86144-067-9
Cover photograph: Jupiter Images

Contents

Introduction

When people mention their blood pressure it is often in relation to it being high. High blood pressure (hypertension) is one of the commonest medical conditions. One in three of us suffer from high blood pressure and millions of people take medications to try to control it. It is much less common for blood pressure to be too low (hypotension), but low blood pressure can occur.

This book is an essential guide for anyone wishing to understand their blood pressure. It takes the reader through what blood pressure is and how blood pressure can be abnormal.

I am a qualified medical doctor and have spent many years working in a hypertension clinic and researching hypertension. From my experience of treating patients, I have first hand knowledge of what many people would like to know about their blood pressure.

Pressure on your GP's time means that they can't always answer all of your questions. This means that when you come out of the GP's surgery armed with a prescription, you probably will not know what the treatment is really for and may wish that there was more time to discuss the details with your GP. This book should be like having your own personal GP with all the time in the world to answer your questions on blood pressure.

All the information in this book is based on the latest evidence from rigorously conducted scientific studies. This information, combined with lifestyle advice and discussions of alternative blood pressure remedies, should mean that by the end of the book you will have enough information to put your own blood pressure plan into action.

'Many people talk about their blood pressure but few of us really understand what blood pressure is, or why it is important.'

Disclaimer

This book is for general information about blood pressure. It is not intended to replace professional medical advice but can be a useful complement to medical advice. Anyone with concerns about their blood pressure is strongly advised to consult their healthcare professional.

Chapter One

What is Blood Pressure?

Your circulation

Your body is made from millions of cells which come together to form your organs. Organs are made up of groups of cells that do similar jobs; your liver, kidneys, brain and heart are all classed as organs. To do the job of keeping you healthy all the cells in these organs need energy and they also need to get rid of any waste products that have built up inside them.

The blood circulating around your body acts as a transport system – it supplies your cells with the glucose and oxygen that they need to make energy and it takes their waste products away.

Your arteries

■ Arteries are blood vessels that take blood away from the heart.

■ Arteries carry blood to other organs in your body.

■ Arteries usually carry blood that is rich in oxygen.

The majority of your arteries carry oxygen-rich blood from the left side of your heart and distribute it to all the cells in your body. The artery that originates in the heart, called the aorta, is very large, but as your arteries extend throughout your body they become much smaller so that they can reach all your cells.

Although most arteries carry blood that contains high levels of oxygen, there are some arteries that transport blood which is low in oxygen. These are the pulmonary arteries which take your blood from your heart to the lungs, where it is topped up with oxygen.

Your veins

- Veins take blood away from other organs.

- Veins bring blood back to your heart.

- Veins usually carry blood which contains low levels of oxygen.

After your cells have taken the oxygen and glucose that they need from your blood, it travels back to your heart via your veins. So, blood in veins usually has much less oxygen than blood in arteries. The only vein that carries blood that is rich in oxygen is the pulmonary vein. This vein brings blood that has been topped up with oxygen in the lungs back to your heart.

Your heart

- Your heart is a muscular pump.

- It has to pump blood up to your brain as well as down to your big toe!

- It is estimated that your heart will beat more than two billion times in your lifetime.

Your heart is basically a muscular pump. It has two sides, a right side and a left side. The right side of your heart receives blood from your veins and pumps this to your lungs where it is topped up with oxygen. Blood from the lungs then flows into the left side of your heart which pumps it around to the rest of your body.

Your heart doesn't just beat at a constant rate throughout your life; it can vary depending on what you are doing. If you are fast asleep your cells, like you, are doing less work than if you are awake. Therefore they need less energy and produce less waste, so when you are asleep your heart doesn't have to pump as much blood to them and it slows down.

When you go for a run, the cells in your leg muscles have to work very hard and need a lot more energy. So, your heart beats faster to supply them with the blood containing oxygen that they need.

'It is often said that members of royal families have blue blood, but the colour of your blood has nothing to do with whether you are royalty. Blue blood just contains less oxygen than bright red blood.'

Your blood pressure

- Blood pressure refers to the pressure of the blood in your arteries.
- The pressure of blood in your veins is not a part of your blood pressure reading.
- Blood pressure is measured in 'millimetres of mercury'.
- Your blood pressure has two components.
- The upper number is the 'systolic' blood pressure.
- The lower number is the 'diastolic' blood pressure.

The pressure in your arteries is created by your heart pumping blood into them, as well as the stiffness of the artery walls. In a central heating system, the amount of pressure needed to force water through the pipes will depend on the size of the pipes. Pipes with a wider diameter will need less pressure than those with a smaller diameter. It is the same with your arteries: if your arteries are stiff and narrow, the pressure needed to force blood through them increases.

While the pump in the central heating system will work at a constant pressure to keep water flowing through the pipes, the pressure system in your body is much more dynamic. Nerves that supply your heart can change both the rate and force of its pumping ability. In addition, nerves that supply your blood vessels can change their diameter. In this way your body can adjust your blood pressure throughout the day. This means your blood pressure is correct for whatever you are doing.

When doctors measure pressure in your arteries they use the units millimetres of mercury (mmHg). This is a standard way of talking about pressure, just like centimetres is a standard way of measuring length.

'Your heart beats on average 70–80 times per minute. It does this every minute of the day for the whole of your life. So to keep you alive your heart has to be the fittest muscle in your body.'

Your blood pressure will usually be written as two numbers, an upper and a lower number. Your doctor will record your blood pressure like a fraction:

upper blood pressure

---

lower blood pressure

Systolic blood pressure – what the upper number means

When your heart pumps blood into your arteries, this increases the pressure within them – just like when you switch your central heating system on, the pump will increase the pressure in your water pipes.

When your heart pumps, it causes the pressure in your arteries to increase to around 120mmHg. This is called the systolic blood pressure and it is the upper blood pressure number that your doctor gives you.

But your blood pressure does not remain at a constant level. Every time your heart pumps, the pressure in your arteries increases to around 120mmHg and then falls again as your heart relaxes. Therefore, the pressure generated by your heart pumping pulsates throughout your circulation, approximately 80 times per minute, and this is what you can feel when you take your pulse.

Diastolic blood pressure – what the lower number means

After your heart has pumped blood into your arteries it relaxes and gets ready for the next beat. When it relaxes, the pressure in your arteries falls. However, it doesn't drop to zero, as blood still needs to flow to your cells when your heart relaxes. The lower pressure in your arteries is called the diastolic blood pressure and is usually around 70mmHg.

The diastolic blood pressure is maintained by the blood within your arteries and the fact that the artery walls have muscle tone and create a pressure of their own.

Normal blood pressure

Your GP may tell you that your blood pressure is normal. Most people will not think any more about this, but working out what a normal blood pressure is has taken many years of scientific study.

How do doctors know what a normal blood pressure is?

The normal curve

Just like people have varying heights, they also have a wide range of different blood pressures. So there is not a single blood pressure that is classed as normal, but a range of both systolic and diastolic blood pressures that are classed as normal.

To calculate this range, over many years scientists have taken the blood pressure of thousands of healthy people. They then plot these readings onto a graph, which looks like a bell and is called a 'bell shaped' or 'normal' curve. The range in the middle of this curve is where most people's blood pressure will lie and is classed as normal.

'To study the abnormal is the best way of understanding the normal.'

William James, American philosopher.

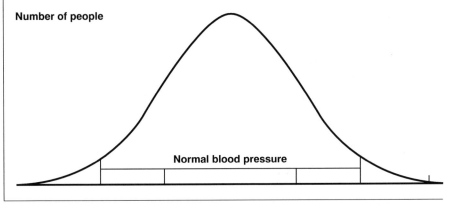

Number of people

Normal blood pressure

Systolic or diastolic blood pressure

The association between blood pressure and disease

However, working out what is a normal blood presssure is more complicated than just plotting a graph, because even though the people used to create this 'normal range' may have been healthy at the time, later on in life they may have developed problems due to their blood pressure.

So, doctors have also taken blood pressure readings from thousands of people and followed them up over time to see whether they develop any problems related to their blood pressure. In this way a normal blood pressure can be classified as one that is less likely to cause illness in later life. The main illnesses that high blood pressure causes are heart attacks, angina and strokes.

What is a normal blood pressure?

- A normal systolic blood pressure is between 90 and 130mmHg.
- A normal diastolic blood pressure is between 60 and 85mmHg.

Do my veins also have a blood pressure?

The blood pressure readings that your GP gives you apply to your arteries. The blood pressure in your veins is much lower – usually around 5 to 7mmHg. Blood is driven via the veins back to the heart mainly by the pressure that your muscles and other organs exert on the veins. One way valves are needed to stop your blood from flowing backwards in veins.

Blood pressure throughout life

Your blood pressure changes on a minute to minute basis, but it also changes throughout your life.

Blood pressure in the growing child

Infants and young children have a lower blood pressure than adults. At birth, a baby's blood pressure is between $^{65\text{-}90}/_{30\text{-}60}$. As children grow up their blood pressure gradually increases to reach adult values at around 18 years old.

Blood pressure during pregnancy

During a normal, healthy pregnancy, the hormone progesterone causes the arteries to relax which means that the heart doesn't have to pump as forcefully to drive blood through them. Therefore, a pregnant woman will usually have a lower blood pressure than normal.

Should my blood pressure increase as I get older?

Blood pressure in people in the Western world often increases as they age. This used to be thought to be normal. However, when scientists studied blood pressure in tribal people who still lived active, hunter-gatherer lifestyles, they found that their blood pressure did not increase with age, even in those who lived into their 70s. In addition, these tribal people didn't suffer from the same blood pressure related diseases as people in the Western world.

It is now thought that Westerners' rise in blood pressure with age is caused by a lack of exercise combined with a poor diet containing too much salt. This increase in blood pressure throughout life is what causes the high amounts of blood pressure related disease in Western society.

Summing Up

Blood pressure is created by the heart pumping blood around your arteries. Blood pressure is low in children and pregnant women, but for the rest of your life your blood pressure should be between $^{90\text{-}130}/_{60\text{-}85}$ mmHg. It should not increase as you get older.

The upper number, or systolic blood pressure, reflects the pumping force of your heart. The lower number, or diastolic blood pressure, reflects the residual pressure in your arteries when your heart muscle is relaxed.

Chapter Two

Measuring Blood Pressure

How is blood pressure measured?

With each heartbeat the pressure in your arteries rapidly rises to the systolic blood pressure before falling to the diastolic blood pressure. So, if your blood pressure is $^{120}/_{80}$, the pressure in your arteries will suddenly increase to 120mmHg and then fall to 80mmHg every time your heart beats, which is usually 80 times per minute.

To measure blood pressure, doctors need to detect both the upper and lower values of this pressure pulsation. They do this using equipment called a 'Sphygmomanometer' which consists of an inflatable arm cuff combined with a manometer, which is an instrument that measures pressure.

Blood pressure is usually measured on your arm, just above the elbow. Here, you have an accessible artery that runs close to your skin, called the brachial artery.

The method of measuring blood pressure is standard all over the world. Therefore, if you have your blood pressure measured in Bangladesh, it should be the same as the measurement in the UK, as long as the equipment used is the same.

Measuring the systolic blood pressure

The cuff which your GP places around your upper arm is inflated to a pressure greater than your systolic blood pressure. This cuts off the blood flowing through your brachial artery to your arm. The pressure in the cuff is then slowly released until it is equal to the systolic blood pressure. At this point blood can again flow through the artery and this pulsation creates a tapping sound that the doctor can hear by listening just above your elbow with a stethoscope. The pressure at which doctors start to hear the pulsation is your systolic blood pressure – the upper number.

Measuring the diastolic blood pressure

Once the systolic number has been recorded your GP will continue to deflate the cuff until the pressure in the cuff falls to just below the diastolic blood pressure. At this point your GP will no longer be able to hear your blood pulsing through your artery. The pressure just before this is your diastolic blood pressure – the lower number.

Machines that measure blood pressure

Old fashioned, manual blood pressure machines use a cuff that has to be pumped up by hand and have a manometer to record pressure. Although this equipment is old fashioned it is very accurate and is the gold standard against which many newer blood pressure machines are compared.

Electronic or digital machines

Newer blood pressure machines are electronic. The cuff is inflated automatically and there is equipment inside the cuff for detecting the sounds without the use of a stethoscope. Some of these machines can also store blood pressure readings so there is a record of how your blood pressure changes over time.

Standardisation of electronic machines

The problem with electronic machines is that there are many makes on the market that are all slightly different in design, which means that the blood pressure numbers that they give can differ. So, your blood pressure could be very different on one machine compared to another.

Some electronic blood pressure monitors have undergone rigorous testing to ensure that the readings given are reliable and the same as would have been given by an old fashioned sphygmomanometer. This means that blood pressure readings taken by your GP, in the old fashioned way, can be compared to those taken by electronic meters.

Some electronic meters are more reliable than others and doctors will only take your blood pressure with the properly tested and reliable meters so they know that any change in blood pressure is a true reading and not just due to a different machine being used.

Measuring blood pressure at home

Why should I measure my own blood pressure?

- Your home blood pressure reading is more indicative of what it is normally like.
- It will get you involved in your own care.
- It is interesting to know how your blood pressure varies throughout the day.
- Patients who take their own blood pressure have better blood pressure control.

Which machine should I buy?

- There are many different machines on the market.
- The prices of machines can vary considerably.
- Some machines are more accurate and reliable than others.

- It can be a false economy to buy a machine just because it is cheap.
- Ask your GP which sort of machine they would recommend for you.

Many people want to measure their own blood pressure. This is usually because they find that their blood pressure at home is much lower than when they are stressed in the GP surgery. You may find that blood pressure readings taken at home give a much better indication of what your blood pressure actually is.

Some people are just interested in how their blood pressure changes throughout the day and buy a machine out of academic interest.

Whatever your reason for buying a machine, when you go into a shop or look online you will be faced with a plethora of machines and choosing one can be difficult.

Is there a recommended machine?

Some home blood pressure monitors are like the old fashioned ones and need you to use a stethoscope. However, because people find these difficult to use, they normally opt for an electronic machine.

Electronic machines that measure blood pressure using a cuff placed around the upper arm are, at the moment, usually more reliable than finger or wrist blood pressure monitors. At present time it is probably better to avoid buying a finger or wrist monitor unless your GP suggests one that is reliable. However, this still leaves many different types of arm blood pressure monitors to choose from.

There are so many machines on the market, is there a way to choose?

What to buy depends on what you are going to use it for and your budget. If you want to compare your blood pressure readings with those your GP takes, it is better if you buy a machine that is known to produce similar readings to the one used by your GP. Your GP should be happy to advise you on this matter.

If you are just buying a machine to see how your blood pressure varies and are only going to be comparing the results with those from the same machine, then the type of machine you buy is less important.

'No matter how relaxing, reassuring and informal your GP tries to be, sitting in a room with someone who knows more about your health than you do can be an understandably worrying experience – enough to put anyone's blood pressure up!'

New machines are often being developed, so for an up-to-date list of recommended machines and their costs see the British Hypertension Society website (see help list).

Is there anything else I need to look for?

The other thing that is important is the size of the cuff. If the cuff doesn't fit you properly, the blood pressure readings will be wrong. Your GP or nurse should be able to advise which cuff size to get.

- Most people will be fine using the standard size cuff that comes with their monitor.
- If your arms are thin and the cuff slips down your arm easily, you will need to get a smaller cuff.
- If you find that you have difficulty doing up the cuff, you may need to get a larger cuff.

How should I measure my blood pressure at home?

Unless your GP has told you otherwise, you should take your blood pressure when you are sitting down with your legs uncrossed. Rest for a couple of minutes beforehand and try not to talk while you are doing it.

The cuff needs to be placed about 2cm above the crease in your elbow. The cuff should fit snugly around your arm, it shouldn't easily slip off and it shouldn't be too tight. Your arm should be resting on a table or desk at the level of your heart while the machine is working.

Before you start taking any readings make sure that you know how to work the machine. Then try it a few times, but don't write the measurements down.

Only start recording your measurements when you are happy using the machine, otherwise stress associated with not knowing how to use the machine will put your blood pressure up.

Step by step guide to taking your blood pressure at home

- Sit down and rest for a couple of minutes.
- Don't cross your legs or talk.
- Place the cuff around your arm, just above your elbow.
- The cuff (when not inflated) should fit snugly around your arm.
- Rest your arm on a table at the level of your heart (just below your nipple).
- When the machine is working try not to move.
- Sometimes the machines will take a while or make a couple of attempts; don't worry if this happens – just be patient.

It is a good idea to get someone in your family to help you use the blood pressure machine at home. It is less awkward for you if someone helps; also, it helps your family to feel involved.

Perhaps someone could help put the cuff on your arm, or write down the readings for you?

When should I measure my blood pressure at home?

Try to pick a few times throughout the day to take your blood pressure. For example, soon after getting up, before lunch and in the evening. Stick to these times (half an hour either side should make no difference) and record your blood pressure for a few days.

Try to capture your normal life when you are recording your blood pressure. If you are on holiday your blood pressure may be much lower than it is at the office, which will give you great readings but not ones that are representative of your true blood pressure for most of your life.

Caffeine can put your blood pressure up, so it is best to avoid coffee for 30 minutes before you plan to take your blood pressure.

How often should I measure my blood pressure?

If you are going to measure your own blood pressure for medical reasons, it is important to do this regularly but not obsessively.

Many people become so worried about their blood pressure that they take hundreds of readings in the hope that they will eventually be normal. As you can imagine, this won't help you relax and may make your blood pressure even worse.

Try to choose certain times on certain days to check your blood pressure and try not to check in between times. If you are unsure when and how often is best, ask your GP or nurse.

Don't forget to write both the systolic and diastolic readings down so both you and your GP can see what is happening to your blood pressure over time.

My GP thinks I may have white coat hypertension, what is this?

For many people, a visit to the GP is a stressful experience. Firstly, you have to get there on time which can be difficult with traffic hold ups. Then you have to try to park at the surgery, and there always seem to be more patients than parking spaces. In addition, just being in a GP's surgery is known to be stressful. So, it is no surprise that some people find that their blood pressure is much higher at the GP's than it is most of the time. The term for this is 'white coat hypertension'.

Some people with white coat hypertension will have perfectly normal blood pressures when they are away from the surgery. Others will still have high blood pressure, but this won't be as marked as it is at the GP's.

If you think that you may have white coat hypertension, it is a good idea to try checking your blood pressure at home. The other good reason to take your blood pressure at home is that it gets you involved in your own health.

What should I do if I think I may have white coat hypertension?

If you think you may have white coat hypertension, mention this to your GP. If they agree with you, they will probably give you a blood pressure monitor to take home so that you can record your own readings.

If you buy your own machine for this purpose, make sure it is one of the recommended and reliable types.

24-hour blood pressure monitoring explained

24-hour blood pressure monitoring is also called 'ambulatory blood pressure monitoring'.

What does this involve?

This involves wearing a machine that monitors your blood pressure for 24 hours. For this a cuff placed around your upper arm is attached to a small monitor that is worn around your waist. The equipment is small and should not prevent you going about your normal daily life.

Sometimes your doctor may just ask you to wear the equipment for 12 rather than 24 hours.

The cuff is programmemed to inflate at regular intervals; usually every 15 minutes during the day and every 30 minutes overnight. It will usually beep before it inflates to give you a warning to sit down and rest your arm before it takes its measurement. Don't worry if you can't sit down, but try to keep your arm still when the machine is working.

Why do I need a 24-hour blood pressure recording?

A 24-hour record of your blood pressure enables your doctor to see exactly what your blood pressure is doing over the whole day.

Reasons for your doctor requesting a 24-hour blood pressure include:

'The inflation of the blood pressure cuff during a 24-hour recording can disturb your sleep. Don't be afraid to tell your doctor if the machine has kept you awake, as they may want to take this into account when they interpret the readings.'

- If your blood pressure readings are slightly raised but your doctor is unsure whether to treat.

- To see if your treatment is working.

- To exclude white coat hypertension.

- To see how your blood pressure varies throughout the day.

Summing Up

Blood pressure can be measured by a variety of machines. The machines can be manual or electronic, but most patients find it easier to use electronic machines. The most important thing about measuring blood pressure is that the readings are accurate and reliable, and readings from different machines can be compared.

Some machines are more reliable than others, in particular, at the present time, most machines that measure blood pressure in your wrist or finger are not as good as ones that measure blood pressure in your upper arm.

Sometimes your GP will need more information than a one-off reading can give, so you may be asked to check your own blood pressure at home, or wear a 24-hour blood pressure monitor. Whenever your blood pressure is being taken, if possible you should sit down with your legs uncrossed and your arm resting on a table at the height of your heart.

Chapter Three

What is Hypertension?

The classification of a normal blood pressure and recommendations for treatment vary slightly between countries. For this reason, reading about the classification of blood pressure on the Internet can become confusing. The numbers quoted in this book are from the British Hypertension Society; an organisation that produces guidelines for the UK. Each country has their own guidelines that may be subtly different from the ones presented here, but the general concepts, as well as the levels of blood pressure that need treatment, are the same in most countries.

High blood pressure

Doctors refer to high blood pressure as hypertension. 'Hyper' means high and 'tension' means pressure.

Your blood pressure can be abnormally high if either the upper (systolic) or lower (diastolic) numbers or both are elevated.

- If only the upper number is elevated this is called 'isolated systolic hypertension'.

- If only the lower number is elevated this is called 'isolated diastolic hypertension'.

- If both are high it is just called 'hypertension'.

'If it weren't for the fact every one of us is slightly abnormal, there wouldn't be any point in giving each person a separate name.'

Ugo Betti, Italian playwright.

The grey areas – raised blood pressure that doesn't require treatment

- A normal blood pressure is classed as being an upper reading of less than 130mmHg and a lower reading of less than 85mmHg.

So I am not at risk from my blood pressure if it is below $^{130}/_{85}$ mmHg?

It is now recognised that as soon as blood pressure rises above $^{115}/_{75}$ the risks associated with having high blood pressure start to increase. However, GPs do not offer treatment for blood pressure of this level because the risks are not great enough to warrant treatment at this stage.

Pre-hypertension

Blood pressures between $^{130\text{-}139}/_{85\text{-}89}$ are now called 'high normal' or 'pre-hypertension'. Blood pressures in this range are associated with a greater risk of heart attacks and strokes, but this risk has to be weighed up against the risks and side effects, as well as costs of treatment. So, on balance, it is thought that pre-hypertension shouldn't be treated.

Many people with pre-hypertension will progress to develop true hypertension which requires treatment, so if you have pre-hypertension your GP will keep a close eye on your blood pressure and ask you to come in for yearly checks.

'For every 20mmHg increase in blood pressure the risk of dying from a heart attack or stroke doubles.'

When does high blood pressure require treatment?

There are three ways in which you can be diagnosed with hypertension:

- If your blood pressure is high on at least three separate visits to your GP.
- If your home blood pressure readings taken on a reliable machine are consistently high.

■ If a 24-hour blood pressure monitor shows your blood pressure is high.

Doctors divide high blood pressure into three main categories; mild, moderate and severe hypertension.

Mild hypertension

Mild hypertension is a blood pressure between $^{140\text{-}159}/_{90\text{-}99}$ mmHg. If your blood pressure is in this range, your GP will start to think about giving you treatment.

Whether or not you need treatment at this stage will depend upon your other risk factors for suffering from heart attacks, angina or strokes later in life. The risk of suffering from these conditions is called 'cardiovascular risk', and high blood pressure is a significant contributor to this risk. If your risk is low (usually said to be less than a one in 10 (or 10%) chance of suffering a heart attack or stroke in the next 10 years), your GP will continue to check your blood pressure and risk every year, but will not offer you treatment.

Your GP will advise treatment if your blood pressure rises above $^{160}/_{100}$ mmHg, or your risk increases to a greater than one in 10 chance of suffering a heart attack or stroke within the next 10 years.

'The American Heart Association estimates that a third of adults have high blood pressure and that, in America, high blood pressure killed over 55,000 people in 2005 alone.'

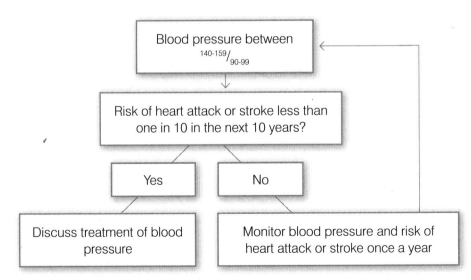

Blood pressure between $^{140\text{-}159}/_{90\text{-}99}$

Risk of heart attack or stroke less than one in 10 in the next 10 years?

Yes

No

Discuss treatment of blood pressure

Monitor blood pressure and risk of heart attack or stroke once a year

I suffer from diabetes, does that make any difference?

If you are diabetic, your risk of suffering a heart attack or stroke is much higher than if you didn't have diabetes. Therefore it is recommended that people with diabetes start treatment for their blood pressure if it rises above $^{140}/_{90}$ regardless of their calculated cardiovascular risk.

How doctors calculate cardiovascular risk

Cardiovascular risk is the chance of suffering from heart attacks, angina or strokes. It is usually given as a percentage over the next 10 years.

There are various different equations that doctors use to calculate this risk. Some of these are available over the Internet and can be found by typing 'cardiovascular risk calculator' into a search engine. Reliable examples are:

- The Framingham risk calculator.
- The ASSIGN score (tailored to a Scottish population).
- Australian absolute cardiovascular risk calculator.

What factors are used in these equations?

- Your systolic blood pressure.
- Your cholesterol.
- Whether you smoke.
- Your age.
- Your sex.

Some will also take into account whether or not you are a diabetic as well as whether your blood pressure has already caused damage to your heart.

Moderate and severe hypertension

- A blood pressure above $^{160}/_{100}$ is classed as moderate hypertension.

Need2Know

However, a slightly elevated blood pressure will not cause any harm and your GP will just keep a close eye on this.

Some definitions of hypertension in pregnancy

Chronic hypertension

This starts before 20 weeks of pregnancy and lasts more than three months after delivery. It is effectively high blood pressure that anyone can suffer from, so, in this case, it just happens to have been picked up during pregnancy.

Gestational hypertension

This develops after 20 weeks of pregnancy and goes away after delivery. In gestational hypertension the pregnancy is the cause of the high blood pressure. However, women who suffer from gestational hypertension are more likely to have high blood pressure later in life.

Pre-eclampsia

This is a combination of high blood pressure and protein in the urine found after 20 weeks of pregnancy. Pre-eclampsia can be mild, moderate or severe. If it is mild, doctors will keep an eye on it. However, in its severe form it can be a serious condition for both mother and baby. Although GPs monitor women's blood pressure during pregnancy and will check the urine for any protein if the blood pressure is raised, pre-eclampsia can also come on suddenly. Therefore if you are pregnant and have any of the following symptoms, contact your GP immediately:

- Blurred vision or loss of vision.
- Severe headaches.
- Nausea.
- Dizziness.
- Pain in the abdomen.
- Sudden weight gain of more than 2lb in a week.

Some of these symptoms are those of a normal pregnancy, but if you notice a sudden change you should contact your GP.

Management of pre-eclampsia

The only way to treat pre-eclampsia is to deliver the baby, and if the baby is developed enough to allow delivery this is what your obstetrician may recommend. If the baby is too immature for delivery, your obstetrician will try to manage the pre-eclampsia until a time when the baby can be safely delivered.

Summing Up

The definition of what is a normal blood pressure varies between countries. In most countries a blood pressure greater than $^{140}/_{90}$ mmHg is considered to be elevated. Whether to treat mildly elevated blood pressure will depend on your other risk factors for heart attacks, angina and strokes. If your blood pressure is greater than $^{160}/_{100}$ mmHg, your GP will advise treatment regardless of your cardiovascular risk.

Blood pressure during pregnancy is usually lower than normal due to the actions of the hormone progesterone. A high blood pressure during pregnancy can have serious consequences for mother and baby and requires the attention of your obstetrician.

Chapter Four

Causes of Hypertension

Primary hypertension

When it comes to high blood pressure, 95 times out of 100 there is no known underlying cause and the high blood pressure is a disease in its own right. This is called 'primary' or 'essential' hypertension.

Just because there is no known cause it doesn't mean that the blood pressure numbers increase all by themselves. High blood pressure occurs in association with many changes in your blood vessels. But finding out whether the high blood pressure or the changes in the blood vessels came first is a little bit like knowing whether the chicken or egg came first.

There are many factors that could put you at risk of developing primary hypertension.

Risk factors for primary hypertension

- Blood relatives who suffer from hypertension.
- Being overweight.
- Excess alcohol intake.
- Excess salt intake.
- Stress.

Having one or more of these risk factors doesn't mean that you will definitely develop hypertension; they just make it more likely that at some point in your life you may develop it.

'When your GP says there is something wrong with you, the logical thing to do is to wonder what the cause is.'

The interaction between hypertension, cholesterol, obesity and diabetes

What is the metabolic syndrome?

The combination of the following is termed the metabolic syndrome:

- Hypertension.
- High cholesterol.
- A tendency towards diabetes (called insulin resistance).
- A leaning towards being overweight, especially if the excess weight is around the abdomen.

Your risk of suffering from heart attacks, angina or strokes is much greater if you have a combination of these problems than if you just have one of them.

If your GP diagnoses you with hypertension they will usually also look to see if you have diabetes or high cholesterol, as treating all of these conditions will reduce your risk of suffering from future heart disease or strokes.

There is some controversy surrounding the metabolic syndrome because doctors don't yet know exactly why these conditions are related. Also, doctors disagree on what to call the combination – some prefer the name 'syndrome X'. Still, no matter what name doctors give to it, there is no doubt that this combination is bad for your health.

'Most cases of high blood pressure have no underlying cause and no overt symptoms. The only way to discover it is by having your blood pressure checked.'

Secondary hypertension

In 5% of cases, hypertension has an underlying cause and is therefore said to be 'secondary' to this cause.

Most of the time if there is an underlying cause this will be obvious to your GP from asking you questions, taking a look at you and performing a few basic blood tests. Therefore, most of the time your GP will not look in detail for underlying causes unless your pressure doesn't respond easily to treatment.

Secondary hypertension can be caused by:

- Medications.
- Hormone diseases.
- Kidney disease.
- Coarctation of the aorta.

Symptoms of secondary hypertension

Just like primary hypertension, there are usually no symptoms of secondary hypertension unless you have symptoms related to the underlying cause.

Medications that cause high blood pressure

Unfortunately, all medications have side effects, but although many drugs cause low blood pressure they do not often cause high blood pressure.

Medications that cause high blood pressure include:

- Some pain-killers.
- Steroids.
- Decongestants.
- Migraine treatments.
- The oral contraceptive pill.
- Some herbal medications.
- Appetite suppressors.
- Recreational drugs.

Most of these medications will not cause you a problem if your blood pressure is normal to start with. If your blood pressure is in the upper range of normal, taking these medications can put it into the 'high' range that needs treatment.

'A combination of diabetes, obesity, high cholesterol and high blood pressure is called "the metabolic syndrome". The increase in prevalence of obesity has made this much more common in recent times.'

Many of these medications can be purchased at a chemist, which means that people often take them without consulting their GP. But, if your blood pressure is known to be either high normal or high, it is best to check with your GP before you regularly take any of these medications.

Pain-killers

The type of pain-killers that cause high blood pressure are called non steroidal anti-inflammatory drugs (NSAIDS). These include ibuprofen, aspirin and Voltarol.

If you have high blood pressure and need to take the occasional pain-killer, try to use paracetamol rather than one of these NSAIDS.

Steroids

Long term steroid treatment causes a condition called Cushing's syndrome. The symptoms of Cushing's syndrome are high blood pressure, an increase in weight, a hump at the top of the back, excess hair growth and stretch marks. If you are on long-term steroid treatment, your GP will regularly monitor you for signs of this syndrome. If you suffer from asthma you may take a regular steroid inhaler. Inhaled steroids are less likely to cause Cushing's syndrome than steroid tablets.

Decongestants

Medications for coughs and colds often contain decongestants. These are adrenaline like substances, for example phenylephrine, which can increase your heart rate and narrow your arteries – both of which result in high blood pressure. However, unless you suffer form severe hypertension it shouldn't be a problem for you to take these tablets.

Migraine treatments

During a migraine, blood vessels in your brain dilate (increase in diameter). Some medications to treat migraines work by narrowing these blood vessels. There are a variety of these medications.

The names for migraine treatments often end in 'triptan', for example: rizatriptan and sumatriptan. 'Triptans' are very effective for treating migraines, but like all medications they have side effects. In particular, they also narrow blood vessels outside the brain, increasing blood pressure.

Appetite suppressants

Drugs to treat obesity by suppressing appetite are often based on a drug called amphetamine, which is also known as the recreational drug 'speed'. Although the amounts of amphetamines in these medications are small, all amphetamine based drugs can increase heart rate and blood pressure.

The oral contraceptive pill

In some women the combined oral contraceptive pill, which contains both oestrogen and progesterone, will cause their blood pressure to increase. This is why if you are on the pill your GP will regularly check your blood pressure.

The oestrogen in the pill is usually the culprit of the high blood pressure. So, if your blood pressure does rise when you're on the pill, your GP will probably suggest switching to the progesterone only pill (known as the mini pill). However, in some women progesterone can also increase blood pressure, so your GP will continue to keep an eye on your blood pressure even when you are on the mini pill.

Herbal medications

Herbal medicines that can increase blood pressure include:

- Ginseng.
- St John's Wort.

- Liquorice.

Herbal medicines, just like prescribed medicines from your GP, can have side effects, and some herbal medicines, for example Ginseng and St John's Wort, can increase blood pressure.

Liquorice can also cause high blood pressure. Liquorice is a component of some herbal medicines and is also found in liquorice sticks and sweets. If you are at risk of hypertension, you should try not to consume too much liquorice.

Recreational drugs

Some recreational drugs, for example cocaine and amphetamines (speed), can have dangerous effects on the blood pressure and heart. Sometimes the increase in blood pressure and heart rate they cause can be fatal.

Hormone diseases and high blood pressure

Hormone diseases rarely cause high blood pressure. They include:

- Diabetes.
- Cushing's syndrome.
- Conn's syndrome.
- Over or under active thyroid.
- Phaeochromocytoma.
- Hyperparathyroidism.

Diabetes

Diabetes is often associated with changes in the blood vessels which makes them stiff and leads to high blood pressure. It can also cause kidney disease, another cause of high blood pressure.

'Although many people take herbal medicines because they believe that they don't have side effects, any medication that has an effect on your body also has the potential to produce side effects.'

Cushing's syndrome

As already discussed, Cushing's syndrome can occur from taking steroid treatments. Steroids are also natural hormones that are produced in your adrenal glands. So, if your adrenal glands produce too much steroid, Cushing's syndrome can be the result.

Conn's syndrome

Conn's syndrome is also called hyperaldosteronism – this means that your body is producing too much (hyper) of the hormone aldosterone (aldosteronism). Aldosterone is produced in the adrenal glands along with cortisol and is responsible for increasing the sodium level in your blood stream. Too much aldosterone causes a high sodium level which in turn leads to high blood pressure.

Over or under active thyroid

Hyper (over active) or hypo (under active) thyroidism can cause either low or high blood pressure. Hyperthyroidism and hypothyroidism occurs when the thyroid gland in your neck produces too much or too little of a hormone called thyroxine.

Symptoms of hyperthyroidism include: rapid heart beat, feeling hot, difficulty sleeping, weight loss and loose bowels. Symptoms of hypothyroidism include: feeling cold, fatigue, weight gain and constipation.

Phaeochromocytoma

A phaeochromocytoma is a growth in the adrenal glands which produces too much of the hormones adrenalin or noradrenalin. These are the hormones that increase your heart rate if you feel stressed. In normal amounts you won't notice any ill effects of these hormones, but if their levels are too high they have a similar effect to decongestant medication. They increase your blood pressure and increase your heart rate. They can also make you feel anxious or agitated.

Hyperparathyroidism

In this condition the parathyroid glands are over active. These glands lie next to the thyroid glands – in medical terminology 'para' means 'next to'. Overactive parathyroid glands result in you having too much calcium in your blood stream. Calcium is similar to sodium in that it increases blood pressure.

Kidney disease and high blood pressure

Kidney disease of any kind can lead to high blood pressure just as high blood pressure can lead to kidney disease. Therefore, if you have kidney disease your GP will keep an eye on your blood pressure, and if you have high blood pressure your GP will keep an eye on your kidney function.

Renovascular hypertension

In this condition the blood vessels ('vascular') supplying one or both of your kidneys ('reno') become narrowed – usually because of fatty deposits that build up in the walls of your arteries (atherosclerosis). This means that not enough blood gets through to your kidneys. Their response to this is to try to increase the blood pressure so that more blood flows to them.

Obesity and high blood pressure

Why do overweight people have higher blood pressure?

Put simply, for people who are the same height, it takes more effort to transport blood round the body of someone who is overweight than someone who is an optimal weight. As your weight increases, your heart and blood vessels have to work harder to supply your cells with the oxygen and nutrients they need. This means that as your weight increases, so does your blood pressure.

Sleep apnoea

Obesity can also cause a condition called sleep apnoea. In sleep apnoea the air passages to the lungs become blocked when you fall asleep. This results in loud snoring but also means that breathing stops completely several times in the night (apnoea means that breathing has stopped). This results in a lack of oxygen in the blood stream which in the long term causes damage to blood vessels and an increase in blood pressure.

Symptoms of sleep apnoea include:

- Loud snoring.
- Times when you stop breathing in the night.
- Sleepiness during the day.

Coarctation of the aorta and high blood pressure

Coarctation of the aorta is a condition in which this main blood vessel, which carries blood from your heart to the rest of the body, is narrowed – this narrowing causes blood pressure, especially in the arms, to increase. It is a condition that people are born with, but may not be detected until much later in life.

Treatment of secondary hypertension

Secondary hypertension usually can be cured by treating the underlying cause.

Summing Up

The most common form of high blood pressure is primary hypertension, where there are risk factors but no underlying causes. Rarely, hypertension has an underlying cause and is termed secondary hypertension. In these cases the high blood pressure usually returns to normal once the underlying cause is treated.

Chapter Five

How Hypertension Affects You

If you are diagnosed with hypertension, you will probably wonder how this is going to affect your health. This chapter will explore the effects of hypertension on your health.

The symptoms of hypertension

No symptoms at all

Most people with high blood pressure do not know that they have it and feel perfectly normal. Therefore hypertension is usually picked up when people pop in to see their GP for some other reason, or as part of a general health check-up.

Does high blood pressure cause nosebleeds?

Many people think that high blood pressure causes nosebleeds, but while this seems logical, most people with nosebleeds have a perfectly normal blood pressure. Nosebleeds are not more common amongst people with high blood pressure.

'Hypertension is a malevolent illness. It lurks silently and without notice, often alerting you to its presence only after its damage has been done.'

How about headaches?

Very high blood pressure, so-called 'malignant hypertension' can cause a headache, blurred vision and even a muddled, muzzy feeling in the head. However, this is very rare and most of the time headaches and muzziness are not due to having high blood pressure.

Why should I worry about my high blood pressure if it causes no symptoms?

This is a common question. The problem is that even though people with high blood pressure feel well, it silently causes damage to organs in their body such as the heart, kidneys, eyes and brain. Because there are no symptoms of high blood pressure, the damage that it causes is often not recognised until it is too late.

The effects of hypertension on the blood vessels

Blood vessels are effectively tubes that carry blood around your body – blood flows through your blood vessels in a similar way to water flowing through pipes. However, unlike pipes, blood vessels are flexible. This means that they can change their shape and adjust the amount of blood flowing through them in response to the needs of your body.

Stiff blood vessels

Just like pipes in a central heating system become damaged when the water pressure is too high, blood vessels can be damaged if blood pressure is too high. Unlike pipes, blood vessels don't usually burst under pressure, but they do stiffen and lose their flexibility under the continual onslaught of blood rushing through them at high pressure.

Atherosclerosis – fatty blood vessels

High blood pressure doesn't just make blood vessels stiff, it can also damage their lining and trigger a process called atherosclerosis – which is similar to a scar forming inside the blood vessel.

Fat builds up in these scarred areas and in doing so makes the centre of the tube become narrow. This makes it difficult for blood to flow through the blood vessel meaning that less blood, and the oxygen that it carries, can get to where it is needed. In severe cases the blood vessel can become blocked by a blood clot, which means that no oxygen at all can get to where it is needed.

Normal artery

Fat starts to build up in artery wall

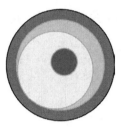

Artery blocked by blood clot

'The term "atheroma" comes from the Greek for a lump of wax. "Sclerosis" is a scar.'

Does atherosclerosis cause symptoms?

Atherosclerosis commonly causes:

- Angina.
- Heart attacks.
- Strokes.
- Leg ulcers.
- Kidney disease.

The symptoms of atherosclerosis vary depending on which part of the body is being starved of oxygen. However, one of the best known symptoms of atherosclerosis is angina, which occurs when the heart doesn't have enough oxygen but there is still some blood getting through the artery. A heart attack or stroke will occur if a blood vessel that supplies the heart or brain becomes completely blocked. We will talk about angina, heart attacks and strokes in the next section.

Hypertension and the heart

Hypertension affects your heart in two main ways. Firstly, it can cause the heart muscle to enlarge. Secondly, blockage to the blood vessels supplying the heart muscle can cause angina and heart attacks.

Enlargement of the heart muscle

Your heart is really just a muscular pump and its job is to pump blood through your blood vessels. High blood pressure means that the pressure in your blood vessels is greater than normal, and your heart has to work harder to pump against this pressure.

When your heart muscle works harder it becomes larger and more muscular. This is similar to the muscle enlargement seen in the arms and legs of somebody who does weights at a gym.

Surely an increase in muscle is a good thing?

Unfortunately, an increase in muscle in your heart (called 'hypertrophy' by doctors) can lead to serious health problems. There are three main problems with an increase in heart muscle, summarised as follows:

- As the heart enlarges it becomes stiff, meaning that it can't pump as effectively as before.

- The extra muscle puts a strain on the nerves that trigger the regular pumping of the heart. If these nerves malfunction the heart can beat irregularly which can be life threatening.

- The extra muscle needs a bigger blood supply, and if the blood vessels supplying the heart can't deliver this extra blood the result is angina.

Angina pectoris

Angina pectoris (abbreviated to angina) is the name given to the pain in the chest caused by a lack of oxygen getting to the heart muscle. This is most commonly due to the blood vessels that supply the heart with oxygen becoming narrowed due to atherosclerosis, but it can also occur if the blood supply to the heart just can't keep up with its demands for oxygen. For example, if the heart is beating very fast, or if it is more muscular than it should be.

Common symptoms of angina

- A heavy or tight feeling in the chest.
- Nausea.
- Breathlessness.

If you suffer from angina and the symptoms don't go away with your normal medication, take it again. If after a few minutes the pain hasn't eased, you should call 999 immediately as you may be suffering from a heart attack.

Heart attack

With angina, the oxygen supply to the heart is reduced but can return to normal. With a heart attack, the blood vessels are totally blocked and oxygen is completely prevented from getting to an area of heart muscle, therefore part of the heart dies.

Symptoms of a heart attack

- A heavy or tight feeling in the chest.
- Nausea and vomiting.
- Breathlessness.
- Sweating.
- Collapse.

'The name "angina" originates from the Greek word for strangling. "Pectoris" comes from the Latin for chest.'

The symptoms of a heart attack may be very similar to a severe angina attack. If you or somebody you know has these symptoms, call 999 immediately so proper treatment can be given quickly.

Hypertension and the brain

High blood pressure puts people at increased risk of suffering a stroke. This is usually because it leads to blockages of the blood vessels that supply the brain. If your brain is starved of oxygen for even a short time, your brain tissue will quickly die.

There are a number of blood vessels that supply different parts of your brain and the symptoms of a stroke will depend on which blood vessel is blocked. If there is a lack of oxygen to the part of your brain that controls movement of your right arm then this arm becomes paralysed. Likewise, if the part of your brain that controls speech is starved of oxygen then this would make it difficult to speak.

- A transient ischaemic attack (TIA) is a stroke lasting for less that 24 hours.

- Many strokes last for more than 24 hours.

- With time and physiotherapy, patients can recover well from a stroke.

- Repeated small strokes over a number of years can cause dementia.

Symptoms of stroke

- Weakness in the face or limbs.

- Sudden inability to find the correct words.

- Jumbled speech.

- Slurred speech

If you or anyone you know has these symptoms, call 999 as soon as possible so that the stroke can be treated.

A useful acronym to help identify that someone may be suffering from a stroke is 'FAST':

- **F**acial weakness.
- **A**rm or leg weakness.
- **S**peech problems.
- **T**ime to call 999.

Hypertension and the eyes

The back of your eye contains a lot of small blood vessels and is the only place in your body where blood vessels can easily be seen.

Hypertension doesn't often cause problems with vision, but if you have hypertension your GP may want to look at the back of your eye to see whether this is affecting your blood vessels.

Hypertension and the kidneys

Your kidneys are the organs that remove many of your body's waste substances. Blood is continuously forced through small blood vessels in the kidneys and waste products are squeezed out of them and into a collection of tubes that join up to drain into your bladder.

In patients with hypertension, the walls of the blood vessels become thick making it difficult for the waste products to be squeezed through them. This means that the kidneys can't remove your waste products efficiently and eventually these build up in your body.

What is renal failure?

Renal failure is when your kidneys don't function properly. In severe cases of renal failure where the waste products in your body have built up to dangerous levels, dialysis is needed. Dialysis basically performs the function of a kidney, filtering waste products from your blood stream.

Usually, high blood pressure is detected and treated a long time before renal failure happens. If your blood pressure is well treated your kidneys will not usually become damaged, but your GP will keep an eye on your kidney function by taking a regular blood test.

Are there other ways in which hypertension affects the kidneys?

The other main way in which hypertension affects the kidneys is by causing atherosclerosis which blocks the large blood vessels that supply them. If this happens, the kidney senses that it doesn't have enough blood flowing through it to remove waste and as a result releases hormones to increase the amount of blood received. The problem is that these hormones increase blood pressure even more. This has also been discussed in chapter 4 under the heading 'renovascular hypertension'.

Can hypertension affect any other part of my body?

Hypertension causes most of its damage by leading to atherosclerosis. The main organs that are affected by this are the heart and brain, but any artery can be affected by atherosclerosis and become blocked. For example, if the arteries to your legs start to become blocked, leg ulcers can result.

My GP talks about cardiovascular disease, what is this?

When doctors refer to cardiovascular disease they are usually referring to disease of the heart and blood vessels due to atherosclerosis (fatty deposits in the arteries). Although hypertension can cause atherosclerosis in all arteries, the main ones that doctors are concerned about are those supplying the heart and brain. Therefore, when doctors talk about cardiovascular disease in relation to hypertension they are, in general, referring to angina, heart attacks and strokes. Sometimes they also include blockages of the arteries supplying the legs and kidneys under the heading cardiovascular disease.

When doctors talk about cardiovascular disease they are usually talking about:

- Heart attacks.

- Angina.

- Strokes.

The aim of treating or preventing hypertension is to reduce your risk of cardiovascular disease (or cardiovascular risk).

Other risk factors for cardiovascular disease

High blood pressure is only one risk factor for all the problems mentioned in this chapter. Other risk factors include:

- High cholesterol.

- Diabetes.

- Smoking.

The risks from high blood pressure are not just added to the risks from these other conditions, they are all multiplied together. So, the resulting risk from having all of these conditions is greater than the sum of the individual risks.

Smoking

Smoking is the biggest contributor to suffering cardiovascular disease and it greatly magnifies the risk from high blood pressure. It is very difficult to give up smoking, but to prevent you suffering from any of these conditions in the future it is important that you try.

'Around one in five people in the UK smoke. Three in five of these would like to give up.'

Summing Up

High blood pressure is not just a couple of abnormal numbers; it is a disease that affects all parts of your body. The problem is that because you can't feel that you have high blood pressure it can cause damage without you even noticing.

High blood pressure is most often thought of as causing heart attacks, angina and strokes; however, it can also damage the kidneys and cause renal failure. Taking treatment to reduce your blood pressure will reduce the risk of these diseases.

If you also suffer from high cholesterol and diabetes, these amplify the risks of high blood pressure and your GP will advise that these are also treated.

Smoking is the biggest culprit of all when it comes to causing heart disease and strokes. Therefore, if you are told you have high blood pressure, diabetes or high cholesterol, it is very important that you try to stop smoking.

Chapter Six

The Causes and Treatment of Low Blood Pressure

When people mention that they have problems with their blood pressure they are usually referring to this being too high, but blood pressure can also be too low. This chapter will discuss what low blood pressure is and whether it is a real problem.

How low is too low?

A low blood pressure is defined as a systolic reading of less than 90mmHg or a diastolic less than 60mmHg.

Many people will be told that their blood pressure is low, but this is usually nothing to worry about, in fact many GPs would say it is something to aim for. In general, the lower your blood pressure, the lower the risk of suffering from a heart attack or a stroke.

Low blood pressure often occurs in people who are fit and active, and they suffer no ill effects of this. Although, some people with a low blood pressure will have symptoms and on rare occasions blood pressure can become dangerously low.

'A low blood pressure is called hypotension. "Hypo" meaning low and "tension" meaning pressure.'

Symptoms of low blood pressure

If your blood pressure is too low, the flow of blood through your arteries to your organs is reduced. Most organs in your body can cope with a reduction in their blood supply for a short time, but your brain can't. Your brain needs more energy than other organs in your body, which means that it needs more blood to deliver oxygen and nutrients than other parts of your body. So, your brain is very sensitive to a reduction in blood pressure.

Most of the symptoms of a low blood pressure result from not enough blood getting to your brain. One of the most common symptoms of a low blood pressure is fainting. In this lying down position blood doesn't have to fight against gravity to return to the heart and from there get to the brain, so blood flow usually recovers rapidly. If someone has fainted and they are left lying down, they will usually recover quickly, although they may feel a little sick and drowsy for a while afterwards.

The symptoms of a low blood pressure are:

- Dizziness.
- Fainting.
- Blurred vision.
- Nausea.
- Feeling cold.
- Lack of concentration.
- Fatigue.

Although these symptoms occur with low blood pressure, they can also occur with other conditions (for example, if you have a cold). Just because you have one or more of these symptoms it doesn't necessarily mean you have low blood pressure.

Is it a fit or a faint?

Sometimes when people faint they can have a few jerky movements of their limbs which onlookers can confuse with a fit. The jerky movements with a faint are usually less prolonged than those with a fit and a faint is not usually accompanied by the other main symptoms of a fit.

Main symptoms of a fit:

▓ Loss of control of the bladder.

▓ Loss of control of the bowels.

▓ Prolonged drowsiness after recovery.

Causes of low blood pressure

Most of the time low blood pressure has no underlying cause and is nothing to worry about; your GP will usually only start looking for a cause if it is causing you problems.

The occasional faint or feeling of dizziness will not usually warrant further investigation, but if these episodes become frequent or start to impact on your ability to go about your normal life, your GP will usually take things further.

Low blood pressure may be due to an underlying condition:

▓ Dehydration.

▓ Infections.

▓ Bleeding/anaemia.

▓ Severe allergy (anaphylaxis).

▓ Pregnancy.

▓ Endocrine (hormone) abnormalities.

▓ Heart disease.

▓ Medications.

'Since Roman times "smelling salts", which release ammonia gas, have been used to bring someone around after they have fainted. They irritate the lining of the nose which stimulates breathing, allegedly resulting in an increase in alertness.'

- ▨ Postural hypotension.
- ▨ Post prandial hypotension.

Dehydration

Dehydration is a common cause of a low blood pressure. Frequent causes of dehydration are:

- ▨ Drinking too little.
- ▨ Vomiting.
- ▨ Diarrhoea.
- ▨ Sunburn.
- ▨ Excess sweating (for example, during exercise).
- ▨ Diuretic medications.

On a hot day it is easy to lose water through sweat without even knowing it. Dehydration is even more pronounced if you are exercising in the heat. It is therefore important to increase your fluid intake on a hot day to avoid becoming dehydrated. But don't just replace the fluid with water – sweat contains salts as well as water, and both need to be replaced at the same time. You also lose salts along with water if you become dehydrated with diarrhoea or vomiting.

If water is replaced independently of salt, the salts that remain in your body become dilute. This can lead to serious illness and many people die from drinking too much water without also replacing salts.

Athletes often drink specially made solutions of water and salts when they are training or competing. You can buy similar solutions from fitness shops or the chemists if you need to replace salt and water after diarrhoea or vomiting. Most people out and about in the heat don't need to buy special solutions but just need to drink juices as well as plain water.

'When you are dehydrated you will usually have lost salts as well as water. It is important to replace both water and salts, and there are special solutions that you can buy to replace both at the same time.'

Infections, bleeding and severe allergy

Other more serious conditions can cause a low blood pressure and will need hospital treatment. These conditions are usually very apparent and both you and your GP will rapidly pick up that you are not well. The exception to this is bleeding. Sometimes blood loss is obvious, but blood can also be lost slowly through the gut or during menstruation in women. In these cases, it is possible to gradually lose quite a lot of blood without noticing and you will only experience symptoms after your blood count has fallen significantly. If your symptoms are due to gradual blood loss, your GP will need to look into the cause before offering treatment. However, if you have lost a lot of blood a transfusion may be advised.

Pregnancy

During pregnancy, changes in the circulatory system occur to make sure enough blood gets through to the growing baby. The main change in blood pressure occurs in the second trimester of pregnancy (12 to 27 weeks), when the hormone progesterone causes this to fall.

Sometimes, when a heavily pregnant woman lies down, her blood pressure can suddenly drop. This is because the weight of a baby in her abdomen puts pressure on one of the large veins that takes blood back to her heart. The vein collapses under this pressure, preventing enough blood from returning to the heart and causing a rapid drop in blood pressure.

To prevent this from occurring, after about 20 weeks into pregnancy, women should not lie down flat and will normally sleep with a pillow under their side. If a pregnant woman faints, they should also have a pillow put underneath one side until they recover.

Anaemia

Anaemia, or a low blood count, usually occurs as a result of blood loss. It can also occur when the bone marrow doesn't produce enough blood cells. There are many reasons for this, but dietary deficiencies of iron or vitamins like B12 or folate are a common cause. If your GP finds that you are anaemic, they will find out the cause behind this before offering you treatment.

Hormone disorders causing low blood pressure

Common hormone disorders that cause a low blood pressure are:

- Diabetes.
- Over or under active thyroid.
- Addison's disease.

It would be unusual for someone who suffers from low blood pressure to be diagnosed with a hormone disorder. Most of the time people with a hormone disorder will know that they have this before a low blood pressure is found. An exception to this is Addison's disease, where the adrenal glands don't produce enough of the hormones that normally keep your blood pressure up. However, your GP will do blood tests to see if you have Addison's disease if your blood pressure is problematic.

Heart disease

Both heart disease and the medications for heart disease can cause a low blood pressure. Heart (or cardiac) failure can often cause low blood pressure. Here the heart muscle becomes weakened and can't generate the force needed to effectively pump blood around the body.

Heart failure often occurs after suffering from heart attacks. It can also happen if your heart beats in an irregular rhythm, or after many years of suffering from high blood pressure.

'The cardinal sign of anaemia is pallor. However, pallor can also be a sign of many other things. Shakespeare seemed to be particularly fond of the word, and used it in his plays to describe many states from anaemia, to shock and even virginity.'

The medications commonly used to treat heart failure can also cause low blood pressure. This means that if you have heart failure your GP will try to balance treating the heart failure with trying to keep your blood pressure up.

Common medications that can cause low blood pressure

- Diuretics (medications that cause water loss and dehydration).
- Any treatment for high blood pressure.
- Some antidepressants.
- Some treatments for schizophrenia.
- Viagra.

Postural hypotension

Postural hypotension means low blood pressure related to posture. A drop in blood pressure when you stand up is very common. You will have probably noticed that sometimes when you stand up too quickly you are suddenly dizzy or get a 'head rush'. This is because the force of gravity means that blood pools in the veins in your legs and less blood flows back to your heart and from there to your brain. Usually, on standing, your body compensates by increasing your heart rate and constricting your arteries to keep your blood pressure normal. But sometimes that doesn't happen quickly enough and the transient lack of blood to your brain makes you feel dizzy.

Postural hypotension is more common in people who are prone to low blood pressure and people over 65 years old.

Post prandial hypotension

'Post' means after and 'prandial' means eating. So, post prandial hypotension means low blood pressure after eating.

When you eat, your stomach and intestines need a high volume of blood to do the job of digesting and absorbing your food. To compensate for this, your body puts the same mechanisms in place as when you stand up – your heart rate will increase and some blood vessels will constrict. But if this doesn't happen to a large enough extent, your blood pressure will drop after eating.

Post prandial hypotension is more common in people who have high blood pressure and people who are on medications for blood pressure.

Investigate how your body tries to prevent postural and post prandial hypotension with your family.

Get someone to take your pulse when you have been lying down for five minutes, then quickly stand up. Give yourself a minute or so and have your pulse taken again – you should find that your pulse rate has increased after standing up. You can also check your pulse before and after eating.

Does my low blood pressure need further investigation?

Low blood pressure only warrants further investigation if it is associated with troublesome symptoms. If your symptoms are just occasional, for example when you are dehydrated or if you have got up too quickly, then your GP will probably not take things any further.

Investigations for low blood pressure

You may already know the reason for your low blood pressure – for example, if you are pregnant, have heart disease or are on medications that lower blood pressure.

If there is no obvious underlying reason, your doctor will examine you and investigate to make sure there is no serious underlying cause.

Investigations that your doctor may do if you have low blood pressure include:

- A heart tracing (ECG).

- A 24-hour blood pressure monitor.

- Blood tests – to look for anaemia and hormone disorders.

- An ultrasound of your heart – to see if it is pumping properly.

- A 24-hour heart tracing – to see if you have any abnormal heart rhythms.

How to treat low blood pressure

Treating low blood pressure usually requires treatment of the underlying cause. For example, if thyroid disease is causing the problem, treating this will bring the blood pressure back to normal. Similarly, if medications are causing the problem, your GP will try to adjust these so your blood pressure returns to normal.

Sometimes, no underlying cause is found, or the cause has no ready treatment.

There are medications that can be used to increase your blood pressure, but, as with all medications, these have side effects and you and your GP will need to work out whether the side effects from the medications are better than suffering symptoms from low blood pressure.

Summing Up

Low blood pressure is usually a good thing unless it causes too many symptoms. The most common symptoms from having low blood pressure are faints and dizziness. In most people, symptoms from low blood pressure are temporary and associated with being dehydrated.

Your GP will look for a cause if your symptoms from low blood pressure are troublesome. Most of the time treating low blood pressure involves finding and treating the cause.

Chapter Seven

Lifestyle Changes to Treat Hypertension

On being told you have hypertension, many questions may run through your mind:

■ What does this mean for the future?

■ Will I have to take medications?

■ How long will I have to take medications for?

■ Can I lead a normal life with hypertension?

■ Is there anything that I can do to change my blood pressure?

This chapter will concentrate on the last two of these questions, in particular lifestyle measures that can reduce your blood pressure. These measures should go hand in hand with the medical treatments that are covered in the next chapter.

Can I still live an active life with hypertension?

YES! In fact, GPs spend a lot of time encouraging people with high blood pressure to become more active.

There is one exception to this general rule and that is if your blood pressure is very high – called 'malignant hypertension'. In this case your GP will recommend that you go into hospital for a period of rest and to start medications to lower your blood pressure.

However, malignant hypertension is very rare and most people with high blood pressure will not need to go into hospital.

If you are diagnosed with high blood pressure, tell your family and try to get them involved in your treatment. This will help them worry less and will make you feel less isolated.

If you live a fit and active life, being told you have high blood pressure shouldn't stop you doing any of your usual activities. However, if you enjoy some sports, like scuba diving, you may need to tell any clubs that you are involved with about your condition. If you scuba dive it is advised that you don't dive unless your blood pressure is well controlled.

'Lack of activity destroys the good condition of every human being, while movement and methodical physical exercise save it and preserve it.'

Plato.

Exercise to reduce blood pressure

One of the risk factors for high blood pressure is a sedentary lifestyle. If you have mild hypertension, you may find that increasing the amount of exercise you do will lower your blood pressure without the need for treatment. Exercise will help you to stay fit and reduce your risk of heart attacks and strokes, even if it doesn't dramatically reduce your blood pressure.

What sort of exercise should I do?

The important thing about exercise is that it is enjoyable. It is no use dragging yourself off to the swimming pool three times a week if you hate getting wet.

- Pick a form of exercise that you think you will enjoy.
- Start off gradually.
- Don't give up.

The problem is that to many people who have got out of the habit, exercise can be a bit of a shock to the system. However, it is surprising how quickly you can incorporate exercise into your daily routine and even to start to enjoy it.

Guidelines state that healthy adults under 65 years old should do either:

- 30 minutes, five days a week of moderate exercise that raises your heart rate and makes you break into a sweat, but allows you to carry on a conversation.

OR

- Vigorous exercise for 20 minutes a day on three days of the week.

If you have not done any exercise for a long time, launching into either of these programmes will be tough, so start gradually, though not so gradually that it is easy to stop. If you are fit and healthy, there is no reason why you can't build up to full strength after a week or two.

It is important not to give up. If you do give up, even for one day, it is easy to sit back in your armchair and forget about your exercise programme. So, don't pick a form of exercise that you are likely to find excuses not to do. If you hate going out in the rain, jogging is probably not the exercise for you. But, if you like social events, why not join a badminton group?

> If you or your parents have high blood pressure, there is a good chance that your children may also develop this condition. To minimise their chance of future problems, get them involved in your exercise programme. If they grow up thinking exercise is normal, they are likely to carry this on throughout life and stay fit and healthy.

'Those who think they have not time for bodily exercise will sooner or later have to find time for illness.'
Edward Stanley.

What if I have other medical conditions?

Usually if you start building up your exercise programme slowly you shouldn't run into any difficulties. But if you are concerned about doing too much too quickly, you have had a heart attack in the past or suffer from angina, it is best to ask your GP for advice.

Smoking and blood pressure

Although you can generally carry on with life as normal if you have high blood pressure, if you smoke you should really consider stopping. The US Surgeon General has called smoking 'the leading preventable cause of disease and deaths in the United States'. The same is true of the UK.

Many people associate smoking with lung cancer, but it is also one of the major causes of cardiovascular disease. If you combine smoking with high blood pressure, your risk of suffering from angina, heart attacks or strokes increases greatly.

In addition, high blood pressure is partly genetic, meaning that if you have high blood pressure your children are more likely to suffer from this later in their lives. Likewise, children who see their parents smoke are more likely to grow up to be smokers. If you have high blood pressure and you smoke, your children are therefore more likely to suffer from cardiovascular disease when they grow up. Apart from encouraging your children to exercise, there is not much you can do about their risk of getting high blood pressure, but by stopping smoking you can certainly help to prevent them taking up this habit when they grow up.

'Smoking takes an average of 10 years off the life span of a person with high blood pressure.'

How to quit

- Give yourself a reason to stop.
- Pick a date.
- Quit with the support of friends.
- Keep away from situations in which you would normally smoke.
- Consider nicotine replacement therapy.
- Ask your GP for advice.

Quitting is difficult and the first step is to find a reason to quit – this could be your health in the future, but doesn't have to be. Other reasons could be your ability to play football at the weekend, your desire to go for a walk without feeling breathless or the future health of your children.

Once you have found this reason, the next thing is to set a date and stick to it. It is sometimes better to get together with a group of friends who also want to quit – then you can support each other.

But perhaps the most important thing, at least for the first few months, is to take yourself away from the situations where you would normally smoke. Often smoking is just as much a habit as an addiction and to break the habit you have to break from your normal smoking pattern. For example, if you normally smoke while having a glass of wine when winding down after a hard day's work then try not to have the glass of wine and find another way of relaxing.

There are also various nicotine replacement therapies, like gum or patches that are very useful in helping people to get over their nicotine addiction. Visit the NHS Smokefree website (see help list) for information on services in your area, or visit your GP.

What to eat to lower your blood pressure

Sodium chloride, or salt, is a major contributor to high blood pressure. We eat salt because it tastes nice, but we don't need any more salt than is contained in a balanced, healthy diet. We certainly don't need to add salt to our food.

It used to be thought that an increase in blood pressure as we aged was normal, but when scientists studied tribal societies in areas like Papua New Guinea, they found there was no increase in blood pressure in the elders of these societies. The reason behind this is thought to be because these tribal people don't add salt to their food. One of the main reasons that Westerners' blood pressure increases as they age is that our diets contain huge amounts of salt, combined with a lack of exercise.

Recommended daily salt intake

- You should consume a total of less than one teaspoon of salt a day (about 2.4 grams).
- You should not need to add any salt to your cooking.
- You should not need to add any salt to food at the table.

Salt is present in all foods – fresh fruit and vegetables, as well as meat, contain sodium chloride. You don't have to add any salt to your food to get enough salt in your diet.

Going salt free

Most people will have got used to a large amount of salt in their diet and will find that cutting this out completely can make their meals taste bland. Rather than go cold turkey, gradually reduce the amount of salt you add to your food, both when you cook and at the table. Eventually, over a period of a few weeks you can reduce the amount of salt to nothing and still have a tasty meal.

Gradually reduce the amount of salt in your whole family's diet. This will be healthier for all of you and it will mean that the person who cooks doesn't have to make separate meals.

Foods to avoid

You should try to gradually cut down on the following:

- Salt.
- Ready prepared meals.
- Processed foods.
- Fatty foods.
- Sugary foods.

Ready prepared meals, processed foods and meals eaten out often have a high salt content to make them taste nicer. Food manufacturers are trying to reduce the amount of salt in their produce and many of them will tell you how much salt their meals contain. However, trying to total up the amount of salt in your food for the day can be complicated, so it is best to try to avoid ready meals or processed food if you can.

Because hypertension is often associated with high cholesterol and diabetes, you should also try to cut down on fatty or sugary foods.

Foods to eat

Basically, you should aim for a healthy diet containing at least five portions of fruit or vegetables per day if you have high blood pressure.

Once you get into the swing of eating healthily it gets easier to prepare tasty meals, but if you need inspiration, there is a diet called the DASH (Dietary Approaches to Stop Hypertension) diet which has been proven in properly conducted scientific studies to reduce blood pressure. If you have mild high blood pressure, following the DASH diet eating plan may stave off treatment. If your hypertension is classed as moderate or severe, the plan may still lower blood pressure and this may be enough to reduce your medications.

See the help list for details of where to find information about the DASH diet.

If you have a family, try to spend at least three nights a week cooking and eating healthy food together. Cooking is a great way of spending time with your family; it will also help to get your kids interested in eating a healthy diet when they get older.

Alcohol and blood pressure

Most people will have heard that a glass of red wine is good for their health, but perhaps not so well known is that alcohol can put your blood pressure up.

If you take no more than the recommended alcohol allowance of 2-3 units per day for women and 3-4 units per day for men, you are unlikely to come to much harm. But higher levels of alcohol consumption can dramatically increase your blood pressure.

If you are a heavy drinker with high blood pressure, reducing the amount you drink to a moderate amount can be almost as effective as taking one of the medications your GP may recommend.

Stress and blood pressure

What is stress?

Doctors use stress to describe an event that triggers an increase in the hormones that your body would normally use to help you get out of a tricky situation. The hormones of this so called 'fight or flight' reaction are called cortisol, adrenalin and noradrenalin. Their role is to get your muscles ready to run by pumping more blood, containing glucose and oxygen, to them.

Non medical people often use the word stress to describe a situation that they have little control over or that worries them in some way. This is quite appropriate because when you feel that you are stressed your body releases the same hormones as it would do if you had to quickly get out of a dangerous situation. The response is the same whether you are being chased by a lion in the African savannah, or being shouted at by your boss.

'Stress is an ignorant state. It believes that everything is an emergency.'

Natalie Goldberg, author of *Wild Mind.*

What have these hormones got to do with blood pressure?

In the short term, the release of these hormones causes your blood pressure to increase. Usually, once the stressful situation is over, the hormones will fall back to normal levels and so will your blood pressure. However, some stressful situations can go on for a long time.

If short term stress puts up blood pressure, can long term stress do the same?

It seems logical that if short term stress can transiently put up blood pressure, long term stress will cause longer lasting high blood pressure – the problem is that this is difficult to prove.

Doctors know that long term stress is associated with hypertension, but whether stress directly causes hypertension is not known. People who are stressed often eat badly, drink too much, are overweight and do little exercise

– all of which are risk factors for hypertension. It is therefore difficult to tease out whether it is the stress or another of these factors that is causing the high blood pressure.

If I have hypertension should I cut down on stressful situations?

Unfortunately, for most people stress is difficult to avoid and it would be artificial to encourage people to avoid stress. However, there are things that you can do to make yourself feel better about yourself and therefore deal with any stress much easier. The most tried and tested of these is doing exercise – regular exercise is a great way of lowering cortisol levels and helping you cope with stress. In addition, eating healthily, drinking less and losing weight will all contribute to you increasing your self-esteem, which will make all situations better to cope with.

Summing Up

Being diagnosed with hypertension comes as a shock to many people, who are often concerned that along with this diagnosis comes a lifetime of taking tablets. However, there are many things that you can do along with your family to try to reduce your blood pressure without going anywhere near a pharmacy.

A combination of regular exercise, eating healthily, drinking less and losing weight will help reduce your blood pressure and may even mean that you don't need treatment. These measures should also reduce your stress levels at the same time as combating your high blood pressure.

Chapter Eight

Treatments for Hypertension

Most people with hypertension feel well; they have no symptoms and usually will not have suffered any ill effects from it. Therefore, if your GP diagnoses you with hypertension, you may be a little reluctant to take treatment and will certainly want more information about the medications recommended. After reading this chapter you should have enough information about the treatments and potential side effects to allow you to enter into a discussion with your GP about what is best for you.

The types of medications for treating hypertension

- The aim of treatment is to reduce your blood pressure to $^{<140}/_{<85.}$
- There are many different types of medication to treat hypertension.
- Some medications will suit some people better than others.

What different types of medication are there?

Medications to treat hypertension are called 'antihypertensive' medications, or 'antihypertensives'. These medications are grouped into categories depending on how they work.

The main categories of medication used to treat blood pressure are as follows:

- Diuretic.
- Beta blocker.
- Calcium channel blocker.
- Angiotensin converting enzyme (ACE) inhibitor.
- Angiotensin II receptor blocker (ARB).

Less commonly used types of medication include:

- Aldosterone antagonist.
- Alpha blocker.

These complicated sounding words actually describe how the drugs work. For example, a beta blocker blocks beta receptors, a calcium channel blocker blocks calcium receptors and an ACE inhibitor inhibits the action of an enzyme (or biological catalyst) called 'angiotensin converting enzyme'.

Nobody will ever expect you to remember these terms, but if your GP refers to your medications by these names (as they often will) at least you will be able to look them up to find out what they do. There is a glossary at the back of this book that provides a short explanation of some medical terms used throughout the book.

Names of medications in each category

All drugs within a category work in a similar way. How these drugs work will be considered later in this chapter, but for now, commonly used drugs in the commonly used categories will be listed, so you can easily check which sort of drug you are on.

Each drug has two names: a generic name that doctors will refer to, and a trade name that the drug companies give their particular version of this drug. Most patients are more familiar with the trade than the generic names.

Only the generic names are listed as some older drugs have different trade names depending on which company makes them. The trade name is usually the largest name on the packet, but the generic name should also be found on the packaging of your medications.

Diuretics

Diuretics in this category are specifically called 'Thiazide diuretics':

- Bendroflumethiazide.
- Hydrochlorothiazide.

Beta blockers

You can tell you are on a beta blocker if your medication ends in the letters '- olol':

- Atenolol.
- Metoprolol.
- Propranolol.

Calcium channel blocks

Calcium channel blockers usually end in '- dipine':

- Amlodipine.
- Nifedipine.
- Felodipine.

But there are some that have unusual endings:

- Diltiazem.
- Verapamil.

'There is no curing a sick man who believes himself to be in health.'

Henri Amiel, Swiss philosopher.

ACE inhibitors

These types of drugs usually end in '- pril':

- Enalapril.
- Perindopril.
- Lisinopril.
- Ramipril.

Angiotensin II receptor blockers

These usually end in '- artan':

- Candesartan.
- Losartan.
- Valsartan.

How do medications to lower blood pressure work?

Each category of drug works in a different way, but many of them relax the walls of your arteries. It is perhaps good to consider the analogy of the central heating system here: it takes a higher pressure to pump fluid through narrow pipes than if the pipes were wider. In simple terms, drugs that relax your arteries effectively widen them, meaning that the pressure needed to pump blood through them falls. Other medications work by helping your kidneys to excrete sodium (a component of salt) and water. Some medications reduce your heart rate. Other medications work by a combination of these actions.

Medications work to lower blood pressure by:

- Relaxing arteries.
- Reducing heart rate.
- Increasing excretion of sodium and water.

Diuretics

Diuretics help your kidneys to excrete sodium into your urine. Water follows sodium into your urine – this is why diuretic tablets make people urinate more often. The loss of salt and water from your blood stream lowers your blood pressure.

Beta blockers

Beta blockers slow down your heart rate as well as relaxing the walls of your arteries.

Calcium channel blockers

Calcium channel blockers reduce blood pressure by relaxing the walls of your arteries. Some of these drugs can put your heart rate up, but some of them don't have much of an effect on heart rate. If your GP thinks that the increase in heart rate will be a problem for you, they will suggest a calcium channel blocker that doesn't have this effect.

ACE inhibitors

ACE inhibitors inhibit the production of hormones that increase blood pressure by narrowing your arteries and getting your kidneys to hang onto sodium. By stopping these hormones being produced, ACE inhibitors relax the walls of your arteries as well as encourage your kidneys to get rid of sodium.

Angiotensin II receptor blockers

These drugs act in a very similar way to ACE inhibitors by relaxing the artery walls as well as encouraging sodium excretion in the kidneys.

Is one tablet better than another?

This is a difficult question to answer. It is known that lowering blood pressure is beneficial. But there is still a lot of debate about whether any one tablet is better than another, even though many studies have been done to try to answer this question.

Although studies haven't found a prize tablet that is better than all the rest, they have found that some tablets may work better in certain people. This has lead to guidelines of which tablets to try in certain people. However, if you are advised to go onto medication, the pragmatic approach is for you and your GP to find a medication that both treats your hypertension and has no (or tolerable) side effects. It may be that you have to try out a few different tablets to achieve this.

'By and large, scientific studies have found that reduction of blood pressure is more important than the type of drug that is used to do this.'

Will I only need one tablet?

Most people get away with just taking one tablet, but some need a combination of tablets. Generally speaking, the higher your blood pressure is to start with, the more likely you are to need more than one tablet.

If your blood pressure isn't too high and the first tablet that you have tried hasn't worked, your GP may suggest swapping you over to a different tablet before adding another one in.

What the guidelines say

Guidelines have been produced for doctors to try to ensure that people get the right treatment for them and that the costs of treatment aren't too high. These guidelines recommend which tablets to start with and also what to try if these don't work.

- ACE inhibitors are the drug of choice if you are younger than 50.

- Diuretics or calcium channel blockers are the drug of choice if you are older than 50 or of African-Caribbean descent.

If your start off medications didn't work, the guidelines suggest that the next step is to try a combination of an ACE inhibitor and a calcium channel blocker, or an ACE inhibitor plus a diuretic.

If taking two medications didn't work, the next step would be to combine an ACE inhibitor with a calcium channel blocker and a diuretic.

	Under 50 years old	Over 50 years old or African-Caribbean
One tablet needed	ACE inhibitor	Diuretic
Two tablets needed	ACE inhibitor + calcium channel blocker OR ACE inhibitor + diuretic	
Three tablets needed	ACE inhibitor + calcium channel blocker + diuretic	

Will my GP always follow these guidelines?

The above guidelines are based on evidence that suggests that these combinations work well. But your GP will know your medical history and may have different suggestions that they think will be more appropriate for you. So, don't be surprised if your GP doesn't strictly follow the guidelines.

Do I need to take hypertension treatment for the rest of my life?

Sometimes lifestyle measures like increasing the amount of exercise that you do or losing weight will mean that your blood pressure falls by itself. Your GP may suggest that you try this initially.

However, if lifestyle changes do not lower your blood pressure enough, you will need medication. High blood pressure can't normally be cured, so when you stop taking the medication, your blood pressure will return to high. This means that you will have to take the treatment for the rest of your life.

Treating isolated systolic hypertension

Isolated systolic hypertension is treated in just the same way as any high blood pressure, with lifestyle modification and drug treatment when required.

If you need to take medications to treat your isolated systolic hypertension, your GP will try to keep your diastolic blood pressure above 70mmHg. This is because there is a concern that a diastolic blood pressure less than 70mmHg can lead to a stroke or heart attack in a person who has isolated systolic hypertension.

Treating isolated diastolic hypertension

There is still a lot of debate amongst doctors about whether to treat isolated diastolic hypertension. The guidelines that doctors work from recommend that they should start to think about offering you treatment for a diastolic blood pressure above 90mmHg. But because the evidence that treatment is beneficial is not strong, you and your GP may decide not to treat your high diastolic blood pressure, especially if you are over 50 years old and have no other risk factors for heart disease or stroke.

If I have hypertension should I also be taking treatment for my cholesterol?

Both hypertension and high cholesterol are risk factors for cardiovascular disease. If you suffer from a combination of high blood pressure and cholesterol, your GP will advise you to take treatments for both.

My cholesterol is normal and my GP has asked me to take treatment – why is this?

It used to be thought that if your cholesterol was normal then you did not need to worry about it. It has now been found that if you have had a heart attack or stroke, or suffer from angina even if your cholesterol is normal, then taking treatment to lower it further is beneficial.

Some doctors also think that even if you haven't suffered from heart disease or strokes but are at a high risk of suffering from these in the future, medications to lower your cholesterol may be beneficial.

There are several different types of cholesterol. Are some better than others?

When people say that their cholesterol is normal they are often talking about their 'total' cholesterol level. But cholesterol isn't just one substance, it is a whole group of substances, some of which are beneficial and some of which are harmful.

- High density lipoprotein, or HDL cholesterol is good.

- Low density lipoprotein, or LDL is bad.

- Triglycerides are bad.

When your GP calculates your risk of suffering from future problems related to your high blood pressure, they will look at how much 'good' and 'bad' cholesterol you have. If you have too much 'bad' cholesterol this will increase your risk and your GP may advise treatment for this – even if your total cholesterol level is normal.

Do all doctors agree that normal cholesterol should be treated?

Most doctors agree that if you have had a heart attack, stroke or suffer from angina then a cholesterol level which is normal should be treated. However, doctors don't agree about whether to treat a normal cholesterol level if you are just at high risk of suffering from these conditions. This is because the lower your cholesterol is, the smaller the benefits to be gained by lowering it even further.

The pragmatic approach that some doctors and patients take is to try treatment; if it works and has no side effects, all well and good, but if it doesn't work or it is not tolerated well, the treatment is stopped.

'Nowadays there is no such thing as a "normal" cholesterol – it is your calculated risk of cardiovascular disease that determines whether or not treatment to lower your cholesterol is advised.'

Side effects of medications and how to deal with them

Unfortunately, all medications that have beneficial effects can also have side effects. This is because no tablet has yet been designed to target the exact cause of the problem – they apply a broad brush approach. This means that they have other effects that may be unrelated to the problem being treated.

Will I suffer from side effects?

Some people tolerate medications better than others. This is nothing to do with stoicism; it is just that some people seem to be more susceptible to side effects.

Most people tolerate blood pressure treatments very well, so it is unlikely that you will have side effects. But, because there are many different categories of tablets to treat hypertension, if you have a side effect with one category of drug it is possible to swap to a different category which may not give you side effects.

What are the side effects?

All of the medications in the different treatment categories have different side effects. There are too many to list here, but some of the more common side effects are:

- Dizziness.
- Low blood pressure.
- Abnormal kidney function.
- High blood potassium level.
- Low blood potassium level.

If necessary, your GP will keep an eye on how your kidneys are functioning as well as your potassium levels by doing regular – usually yearly – blood tests.

'There are no side effects – only effects. Those we thought of in advance, the ones we like, we call the main, or intended effects, and take credit for them. The ones we didn't anticipate, the ones that came around and bit us in the rear – those are the "side effects".'

John D. Sterman, Massachusetts Institute of Technology.

There are so many side effects listed in my patient information leaflet – should I be worried?

All medications in the UK come with a patient information leaflet inside the packet. It is a good idea to have a look through this leaflet to check that you don't have any of the conditions where you should not take the particular medication. However, it is not a good idea to worry too much about the side effects that are listed unless you suffer from an effect that you think may be due to the medicine. In which case, check the leaflet to see if the symptoms that you are suffering from could be due to your treatment. If so, contact your GP immediately.

Drug companies are obliged to list all of the potential side effects of a medicine, but this doesn't mean that you are likely to suffer from any of these.

What should I do if I suffer from a side effect?

If after starting to take your medications you notice something wrong, it is always a good idea to talk to your GP about this. Usually, side effects are nothing to worry about and, if they don't bother you too much, you can just carry on as normal. If they are troublesome to you it is worth discussing a change of tablet with your GP.

Another idea is to change the time that you take your tablet. Sometimes, taking your medication before you go to bed means that you may sleep through the worst of the side effects. However, do check with your GP if this is a good idea for the particular medication you are on.

On very rare occasions, side effects can be serious and need further investigation by your GP.

Summing Up

There are many different types of medication to treat high blood pressure. If you need treatment, your GP will advise you on which one is best based on knowledge of any other medical problems that you may have, as well as current recommendations.

Whether you need to take more than one tablet will depend on how high your blood pressure is and how well it responds to the first treatment. Most people with high blood pressure only need to take one tablet, but unfortunately treatment is usually for life. However, lifestyle changes can cause blood pressure to fall.

All tablets have side effects but some people seem to be more susceptible to these than others. If you do suffer from a side effect of your medications let your GP know – they may be able to swap you onto a tablet that suits you better.

Chapter Nine

Balancing the Risks and Benefits of Hypertension Treatment

Most people are not keen to take tablets. If your GP advises you that your high blood pressure needs treatment, it is therefore understandable that you may want to take some time to think about this. You will not be alone if you want time to consider whether to take a tablet that may give you side effects to treat a condition that – at the moment – does not make you feel unwell.

For everything in life there are risks as well as benefits and most big decisions that we make are based on balancing these; if it turns out that we think the benefits are greater than the risks we will go ahead.

Decisions to take tablets are also made by balancing the benefits against the risks. However, with medications, doctors and medical scientists have done the ground work – they have worked out the benefits and the risks of taking tablets during scientific studies involving large numbers of patients.

> 'Nothing will ever be attempted if all possible objections must be first overcome.'
> Samuel Johnson, author.

Should I do what my GP says and take the tablets?

When your GP advises you to take a tablet, this advice will be based on them having calculated that, for you, the benefits outweigh the risk. The problem is that your GP is not the person that has to take the tablets, you are. Although your GP is trying to make the best decision for you, you may wish to enter into a more balanced discussion with your GP about this decision. After reading this chapter you should have enough information to enter into this discussion.

The medical risk: benefit ratio

Every decision that a doctor makes about caring for their patients involves thinking about the balance between the risks and the benefits. Doctors have to consider the risks of the disease running its course without treatment, as well as the risks of treatment. Because treatments don't usually fully prevent a disease from running its course, doctors also need to consider how much of a benefit a treatment is likely to have.

In weighing up risks and benefits of treatment, doctors consider:

- Risks associated with the disease.
- Benefits of treatment.
- Risks of treatment.

If a medication is beneficial and doctors think that the risks of taking this treatment are less than the risks of letting the disease run its course, they will advise that you take the treatment.

'And the day came when the risk to remain tight in a bud was more painful than the risk it took to blossom.'

Anais Nin, writer.

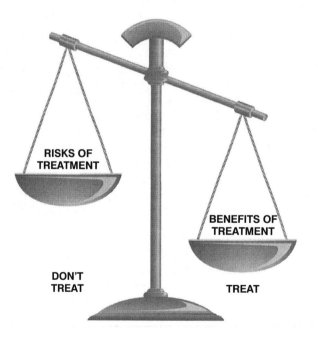

RISKS OF TREATMENT

BENEFITS OF TREATMENT

DON'T TREAT

TREAT

The risks of not treating high blood pressure

The risks of not treating high blood pressure and letting it run its course have been outlined in chapter 5.

In summary, if high blood pressure runs its course, you are at a greater risk of suffering from:

- Heart attacks.
- Angina.
- Strokes.
- Other blood vessel diseases.
- Kidney disease.

This does not mean that you will definitely suffer from these conditions if you don't treat your high blood pressure, just that they are more likely.

The combination of hypertension and diabetes or high cholesterol puts you at an even greater risk of the above conditions.

The most common conditions attributed to hypertension are heart attacks, angina and stroke. Therefore, treatment for high blood pressure is given with the aim of minimising the risk of these conditions occurring.

How these risks are calculated

Doctors calculate your future risk of suffering from a heart attack, angina or stroke using a cardiovascular risk calculator. As risk can vary depending on which country you live in, your doctor will use the most appropriate risk calculator for you. However, to get a rough idea of your risk these risk calculators can be accessed over the Internet.

How risk is calculated has been covered in detail in chapter 3. In summary, the calculator takes into account factors such as your age, sex, blood pressure, cholesterol and whether you have diabetes. Based on this information it gives a percentage risk of you suffering from a heart attack, angina or stroke in the next 10 years.

What does this figure really mean?

Simply speaking, if your risk is calculated to be 10% over the next 10 years, this means that you have a one in 10 chance of suffering from the adverse consequences of high blood pressure in the next 10 years.

It is sometimes easier to think about this as follows. If there were 10 people who all had the same risk as you (the same blood pressure, age, sex, cholesterol and history of diabetes) then one of them would suffer from a heart attack, angina or stroke in the course of the next 10 years.

If you turn this on its head it means that if you don't take treatment for your hypertension you have a 90% (or nine out of 10) chance of remaining well.

These are just numbers, what do they translate to in health terms?

A one in 10 chance of suffering from the adverse consequences of hypertension seems small. But if you are unlucky enough to suffer from a heart attack, angina or stroke, this can have a large impact on your life. All of these conditions can be disabling or even life threatening and all require treatment, meaning that the stakes in this particular risk benefit calculation are quite high.

The benefits of treating hypertension

The benefits of taking treatment for high blood pressure come from a reduction in the risk of suffering from cardiovascular disease in the future. Treating hypertension will not make you feel any better right now.

How much will treatment reduce my risk by?

This is difficult to answer exactly as it all depends on how much of an effect the treatment has on your blood pressure. The greater the reduction in blood pressure, the greater the reduction in risk. If the treatment lowers your systolic blood pressure by 6mmHg, this will reduce your risk more than if the treatment only lowers your blood pressure by 3mmHg.

90

A good way of calculating how much your risk has decreased by is to firstly record your calculated risk before treatment and compare this to your risk once your blood pressure has fallen. If you have computer savvy kids they can help you with this.

A rough guide is that a blood pressure fall of 5-6mmHg will reduce your risk of a heart attack by around 20%.

It seems that the benefits from treatment are large, are my calculations correct?

A 20% reduction in risk sounds quite large, but it is not quite as good as it initially seems.

If you start with a 10% risk of cardiovascular disease in the next 10 years, reducing this by 20% still leaves you with a risk of 8%.

Think of it as follows:

20% of 10% equals 2%. This means that if your risk is 10% to start with, reducing this by 20% actually translates to a reduction in your risk of 2%.

10% minus 2% leaves you with an 8% risk.

Putting this another way, if your risk of a heart attack in the next 10 years is one in 10, taking treatment to reduce this by 20% will still mean your risk is still 0.8 in 10 – which is pretty close to one in 10.

This number seems pretty small, is it worth taking the treatment?

This is very much a personal choice. Most GPs would advise that you do take treatment as they know that the stakes are high and that even a 2% reduction in your risk of suffering from a heart attack is worth trying to achieve. However, there are also risks and side effects of taking the tablets that need to be balanced against the benefits gained from reducing high blood pressure.

The risks of treatment

Most treatments for high blood pressure don't have any serious side effects. However, some tablets can cause your potassium levels to become too high or too low. Also, the tablets can sometimes cause kidney problems. Your GP will regularly take blood tests to monitor your potassium levels and kidney function if you are on the sort of tablets that have these side effects.

Despite the fact that the majority of people will not have any serious side effects, some people do find that the tablets make them feel generally unwell.

How do I work out whether to take treatment or not?

Both you and your GP need to work out your risks and benefits of taking medication to lower your blood pressure.

You will need to consider the risks of not treating your high blood pressure:

- Untreated hypertension puts you at risk of future heart attacks, angina and strokes.

- Heart attacks, angina and strokes are potentially life threatening and require lifelong treatment.

You will need to consider the benefits of not treating your high blood pressure:

- By itself hypertension does not make you feel unwell.

You will need to consider the benefits of treatment:

- By reducing blood pressure, treatment for hypertension reduces your risk of future heart attacks, angina or strokes.

You will need to consider the risks of treatment:

- Although there is a very small risk of serious side effects with treatment, some people find that treatment makes them feel unwell.

This all seems a bit overwhelming, is there a simple answer?

You do not have to make a decision on whether to take tablets for your high blood pressure by yourself. Your GP has had much more experience of calculating the risks and benefits of treatment and will be happy to talk to you about this if you are worried.

Unfortunately, there is no simple answer as to whether it is going to be beneficial for you to take medication for your blood pressure. However, a pragmatic approach to think about is as follows:

- If you do suffer from a consequence of hypertension, this can be life threatening.

- So, even though treatment only reduces the risk of these consequences by a small amount, it is probably worth trying to take treatment.

- If the medication works and doesn't cause you any ill effects, then it is worth carrying on with it.

- If the medication causes you side effects and affects your quality of life, you may want to consider whether it is worth continuing to take it.

If you do want to stop taking your medication, always discuss this with your GP.

Summing Up

Whether or not to take a medication is very much a personal choice. Your GP will offer you sound advice but in the end it is you who will be taking the tablets rather than your GP.

As with everything in life, taking tablets entails benefits and risks. Certainly, reducing the possibility of suffering from a serious consequence of hypertension is worthwhile, but tablets will not reduce this possibility by a large amount. If the tablets affect your quality of life, you may not wish to take them.

Most medical practitioners will advise you to take medications to lower your blood pressure as long as they don't give you side effects, or you are able to tolerate the side effects.

Chapter Ten

Non Medical Remedies for Hypertension

After being diagnosed with high blood pressure, a lot of patients explore non-prescription therapies. The methods that they explore include herbal remedies, acupuncture and relaxation therapies.

Some of these therapies may help. However, unlike prescription medicines, none of these methods have been tested in large trials involving thousands of patients. Until alternative remedies have undergone such rigorous testing they should not be seen as a replacement for medical treatments for hypertension.

Relaxation therapies

- In the short term, stress can cause high blood pressure.
- Long term stress is associated with high blood pressure.
- It is not known if long term stress causes high blood pressure.
- Relaxation techniques may help to lower blood pressure.

Stress and high blood pressure go together. Even though stress may not directly cause high blood pressure, it is associated with poor eating habits, obesity, smoking and high alcohol intake – all things that can put your blood pressure up as well as lead to cardiovascular disease. However, there is some evidence that relaxation techniques may reduce blood pressure.

A thorough review of relaxation therapies is beyond the scope of this book, but overleaf is a very brief description of ones that have been looked at for treating hypertension.

- Autogenic training (training yourself to think about your breathing or heartbeat).

- Cognitive behavioural therapy or CBT (aiming to change the way you think about situations).

- Meditation.

- Guided imagery (focusing on relaxing images).

- Biofeedback (training yourself to lower your own blood pressure).

- Progressive muscle relaxation (concentrating on relaxing different muscle groups).

- Yoga.

Do I need to be trained in any of these methods?

Ideally, yes. All of these methods are intended for you to be able to do on your own, but there is a learning curve for most of them and you will probably need to be taught the techniques by a certified practitioner.

Are any methods better than others?

Basically, when you are trying to relax, the technique that works for you is a very personal thing. However, in studies that have looked at relaxation techniques for treating blood pressure, the ones that have worked best are:

- Progressive muscle relaxation.

- Biofeedback.

- Cognitive behavioural therapy.

How do I choose which method to try?

Knowing which, if any, method will work for you is often a matter of giving a few a try and seeing if they have beneficial effects. You will need to be objective about the length of time you are going to give a treatment to see if it works. It is no use continuing to try different techniques in the hope that one will eventually work, while in the mean time your blood pressure is going untreated.

Chiropractic manipulation

Spinal manipulation has been offered for a variety of different complaints in recent years. Some chiropractors have suggested that it may be useful for treating high blood pressure. However, studies in a large number of patients have not consistently shown any benefit of chiropractic manipulation on blood pressure.

Herbal remedies

People often make a distinction between prescription and herbal medicines. They think of prescription medicines being produced by chemists in a lab, whereas herbal medicines are collected by botanists. However, there is more overlap than is realised. Many medicines that are prescribed by doctors have come from plants and fungi. For example, digoxin, used to treat abnormal heart rhythms, comes from the foxglove, and some treatments for migraine come from fungi. Herbal remedies that work well against disease are usually incorporated into mainstream medicine, while those that work less well remain as herbal remedies. This is not to say that they have absolutely no effect, just that there are often better, tried and tested mainstream medicines available.

Are there any herbal remedies that treat hypertension?

The following herbal remedies are amongst those suggested to be beneficial in treating hypertension:

- *Arnica montana*.

- *Aurum muriaticum.*
- *Ignatia amara.*
- *Natrum muriaticum.*
- *Secale cornatum.*
- *Veratrum album.*
- *Valeriana officinalis.*

There are many others that can be added to the list. The only two of the above that have scientifically shown some promise for treating hypertension are *Secale cornatum* and *Veratrum album*. However, there have been no large trials showing convincing evidence that any of these treatments reduce blood pressure.

But herbal medicines don't have side effects. So aren't they better than prescribed medicines?

Although herbal medicines may not have severe side effects, some of them do have unwanted effects and they can also interact with any prescribed medications that you are on.

If you do decide to try a herbal remedy for your blood pressure, check with your GP that it is not going to react or interfere with any of your other medications.

Should I avoid herbal medications for treating my blood pressure?

Whether or not to try herbal medicines is a matter for you to decide. However, when making up your mind about whether to try herbal remedies for your blood pressure you should consider the following:

- There is no convincing evidence that herbal remedies work well in treating high blood pressure.
- There is good evidence that prescribed medicines reduce blood pressure.

I have heard about Coenzyme Q10. Can this help my blood pressure?

Coenzyme Q10 is found in most plant and animal cells. It is being looked at by scientists as a potential therapy for a variety of conditions and high blood pressure is one of these. There is some good evidence that Coenzyme Q10 may have a blood pressure lowering effect, but it has not yet been properly compared to conventional medicines for high blood pressure.

Acupuncture

There have been a few small studies looking at whether acupuncture can lower blood pressure. Some of them have shown good results, but others have not. So far the jury is out on acupuncture.

Can alternative treatments work at all?

Many people swear by alternative treatments, especially if they have found one that has worked particularly well for them. The problem is that just because a therapy has worked well for one person, it does not mean that it will work well in everybody. It may even be that the therapy didn't really work in the one person that is supporting it – their blood pressure may have fallen for a reason completely unrelated to the therapy.

How do doctors test to see if medicines work?

When doctors think a therapy may be beneficial, they compare it to a placebo (or sham treatment) in many people. For them to say that the treatment works, it has to be better than the placebo in a significant number of these people.

If there are already therapies that are known to be good at treating diseases, any new therapy has to be tested against the best treatments that are already available. If it is as good as, or better than these, it will find its way into mainstream medicine.

'Acupuncture is a traditional Chinese medicine. It involves inserting fine needles into the skin at specific points, or meridians, where "qi" (life energy) is supposed to flow.'

Have alternative treatments been tested in this way?

Many alternative treatments have been tested against a placebo in small numbers of patients. Most of them haven't shown any benefit. The few that have, like Coenzyme Q10, are being further investigated.

The risks of alternative treatments

The main risk of taking an alternative treatment is that you will not seek medical help and in turn won't be prescribed a medication that is known to be beneficial.

Most of the time there is no harm in taking alternative treatments as long as you keep liaising with your GP. If the alternative treatment is not helping you, they will recommend that you take a prescribed medication.

'If your blood pressure is dangerously high, the sensible path is to take prescribed medications that are well known to treat high blood pressure.'

Summing Up

There are many alternative remedies that are promoted for hypertension. Most of them have not been scientifically studied and there is no evidence to say that they work. Of the ones that have been scientifically studied, many have not been shown to be effective. There are a few, however, (for example: relaxation therapies and Coenzyme Q10) that show promise.

If you have moderate or severely high blood pressure then most doctors would recommend that you take a prescribed treatment for this. If your blood pressure is mildly elevated, most doctors wouldn't disagree with you if you were to try alternative therapies in the first instance, before thinking about taking medications if alternatives didn't work.

For more specific information on stress, see *Stress – The Essential Guide* (Need2Know).

Chapter Eleven

Your Personal Plan for Tackling Hypertension

You should now have a better understanding of what blood pressure is, and how high blood pressure can be detrimental to your future health. To avoid the ill effects of hypertension, the best plan is to get together an action plan to avoid getting hypertension at all. The earlier you can do this, the better. However, all is not lost if you already have hypertension. An action plan may reduce your blood pressure to normal, but even if it doesn't, lowering your blood pressure by a small amount will help to protect you against cardiovascular disease.

There have been many suggestions throughout this book about how to combat high blood pressure. Here these suggestions will be brought together to help you create your own personal plan for tackling high blood pressure.

As hypertension is just one factor that contributes to heart attacks, angina and strokes, your personal plan to tackle hypertension should also take into account other risk factors for these diseases. Therefore, as part of this action plan you should ideally include plans to eat healthily and to stop smoking.

'Knowledge is power, and power will enable you to change.'

If you have a young family it is ideal to get them involved in your plan because if they can get used to a healthy lifestyle they are less likely to suffer from hypertension later in life. Also, if you can, encourage your family to join in with your action plan – it will be much more fun for you!

An exercise programme

Exercise will both reduce your blood pressure and generally reduce your risk of suffering from heart attacks, angina and strokes.

At the end of the day most people, whether they have been at work, school or are retired, feel exhausted. Often the monotony of doing the same thing each day can cause mental fatigue that permeates the whole of your body, leaving you wanting to do no more than sit on the sofa.

Although you may not believe this, after you have got used to it, an exercise programme will make you feel so much more alert and awake. Doing regular exercise will also help you to sleep well and combat stress.

Devoting 20-30 minutes to exercise everyday will make you feel and function so much better!

How to plan your fitness programme

- Write your plan down. Think about what sort of exercise you enjoy doing. If it has been a while since you did any exercise, think back to what you used to enjoy.

- If you have children, think about whether it is possible to get them to exercise with you. But remember that young children will not be able to exercise as vigorously as you, so you may need to incorporate them into just small parts of your exercise routine.

- Do you have friends who you could exercise with? Think about getting together as a group; this will increase your motivation and make the whole process more fun.

- Join a club. If you don't think you will have the motivation to exercise by yourself and can't persuade your friends to join you, think about joining a club. The sort of clubs that are useful are not gyms, but clubs where you have to interact with other people and your presence is missed if you don't turn up. For example, a badminton club, or a running group.

- Set a date, write it down and sign it. If you write the date that you are going to exercise and the length of time you will exercise for, in a prominent place where everyone can see it, you may be more likely to stick to it.

- Build up gradually. Underneath your exercise start date write down subsequent dates that you are going to exercise on, but make sure to build up the time that you exercise gradually, over a couple of weeks or so.

- Keep a diary. Every time you exercise write what you did and how long for in an exercise diary or spreadsheet. It is also a good idea to write how you felt after each session. This will help you to see how you are improving; it will also help you to see when you have missed too many sessions.

- Don't give up. The first couple of weeks of any exercise programme are the hardest, but if you can persevere it will get easier.

Changing your diet

Reducing the amount of salt in your diet and losing any excess pounds will help to combat hypertension. But there are additional dietary measures – for example, cutting down on fatty or sugary foods, and eating more fruit and vegetables – that will lower your risk of cardiovascular disease in ways other than by lowering your blood pressure. It is ideal if you can modify what you eat to promote general fitness of your heart and arteries, as well as specifically trying to tackle your blood pressure.

In a time-pressured society, it is all too easy to eat on the hoof and not think too much about what you are actually eating. However, if you are worried about your blood pressure, it is important to try to start to eat healthily. Also, if you have children, getting them to think that healthy eating is normal will be of huge benefit to them later in life.

Losing weight

Being overweight puts you at risk of:

- Hypertension.

- Diabetes.

- High cholesterol.

If you are overweight, for the sake of your health, you should think about losing a few pounds.

I don't eat much, am I overweight because I have a slow metabolism?

It isn't usually the case that an overweight person's metabolism is slow. If you are overweight it means that you are eating too much and/or not expending enough energy throughout the day to burn off excess calories.

I have tried many diets but they never work

There are many different diets to try, some of which advertise miracle results. However, the sensible approach is to just try to gradually cut down the amount that you eat. A small reduction in food at meal times, combined with cutting out snacks between meals, is a sustainable approach that won't leave you ravenous. This approach is more likely to work than a fad diet.

Will exercise help me to lose weight?

Weight loss is most successful when a healthy diet is combined with exercise. Exercise will help you to keep the weight off once you have lost it, so it is ideal to start to diet and exercise at the same time.

Changing the food that you eat

As discussed in chapter 7, a low salt diet can dramatically improve your blood pressure, and a healthy diet rich in fruit and vegetables will help to protect you against heart disease and strokes. Even if you are not overweight, a change in your diet to include more healthy types of food can be very beneficial.

The DASH diet (see help list) has many healthy eating and low salt recipes that you may want to try out. However, with the help of a normal cookbook you can also pick recipes that contain fruit and vegetables, are low in fat and don't require you to add salt.

How to change your diet

- Record what you normally eat every day, for two or three days. Save this record for later comparison.

- Look at this list and work out where you can swap an unhealthy for a healthy option, for example a chocolate bar for a fruit bar or a bag of chips for a baked potato.

- Plan to eat at least five portions of fruit and vegetables each day. This sounds a lot, but don't forget things like fruit juice count as a portion. Write down how you are going to achieve this.

- Pick a few evenings in the week where you and your family can cook and eat a healthy recipe together.

- Gradually, over the course of a couple of weeks, reduce the amount of salt you add to your food.

- Try not to buy too many ready prepared meals or, if you do buy these meals, check to see that they are low salt, healthy options.

- At the end of each month record what you eat for a few days to see where you have improved and also where you can make more improvements for the next month.

Should I take antioxidant vitamins?

Many people think that antioxidant vitamin supplements are a useful part of a healthy diet. Unfortunately, there is no evidence to suggest that this is correct. Although these substances are beneficial when they are contained in vegetables, scientific studies have shown that they lose their benefit when they are taken as pills. In fact, antioxidants taken as vitamin pills may actually be harmful.

The best way to make sure that you take in the right amount of vitamins is to eat a healthy and balanced diet.

Cutting down on alcohol

	Women	Men
Weekly alcohol allowance	21 units	28 units
Daily alcohol allowance	2-3 units	3-4 units

Excessive amounts of alcohol can increase your blood pressure, as well as cause liver disease, stomach ulcers and contribute to many other medical conditions. For most people, sticking to the daily recommended amount is not going to cause any harm. But, drinking more than this amount could lead to future health problems and could contribute to high blood pressure.

'If we see you smoking we will assume you are on fire and take appropriate action.'

Douglas Adams, author.

Stopping smoking

Smoking doesn't directly cause high blood pressure, but it is a huge risk factor for developing heart disease or strokes. Any action plan to tackle hypertension should ideally include a plan to stop smoking as part of a general aim to reduce this risk.

Stopping smoking has been covered in detail in chapter 7. However, if you smoke, you will need to plan to incorporate quitting into your personal plan for tackling hypertension.

Make a contract with your family. Write the date that you are going to stop on a piece of paper in big letters, sign it and put it where your family can see it.

Smoking is an addiction and it is very easy to keep finding excuses not to give up this habit. Do words like 'I will do it after my interview' or 'after the kids have started back to school' or 'after the weekend' sound familiar?

Choose when to incorporate quitting into your plan carefully. Some people like to turn over a new leaf all at once. However, if you try to make too many changes to your lifestyle all at once, you may find it is too much to cope with. Be successful in changing one thing before moving on to another.

As smoking is a large risk factor for heart disease and strokes, it may be the thing that your GP suggests you do as the first part of your plan. In which case, once you have quit don't forget to put the other parts of your personal plan into action.

How to quit

This was covered in chapter 7, but some pointers to refresh your memory are as follows:

- Give yourself a reason to stop.
- Pick a date.
- Quit with the help of friends who also wish to stop smoking.
- Keep away from situations in which you would normally smoke.
- Consider nicotine replacement therapy.
- Ask your GP for advice.

'You will always find a reason to delay quitting, so you need to make a date to stop and stick to it – no excuses.'

A partnership with your GP

Your GP's job is to keep you fit and healthy. This should be your priority also. Keeping your blood pressure low should be something for both you and your GP to aim for. The best way to ensure that both of you get your wish is to form a partnership to achieve these ends.

Your GP will be delighted if you are taking an active part in taking care of yourself, but don't forget that your GP is a valuable source of information. Combining your effort with the knowledge of your GP is the best way of ensuring you remain fit and healthy.

If you have high blood pressure, when you see your GP mention that you want to take an active part in trying to lower this:

- Ask them about weight loss or for healthy eating information.
- Ask them about recommended exercise programmes for you.
- Ask them about stopping smoking.
- Ask them about whether your alcohol intake should be reduced.

Your GP may also be able to advise you of local groups to help with these aims.

But don't forget, while you will probably be impatient to see your blood pressure fall, your GP will know that these things take time. Don't be frustrated if things aren't improving as quickly as you would like.

Summing Up

Your health is in your hands. GPs can give you tablets to treat your blood pressure, but it is much better to develop your own personal plan to tackle hypertension, so your blood pressure doesn't become elevated in the first place.

If your blood pressure is normal, putting the suggestions in this chapter into action will reduce your risk of ever having to take tablets for hypertension. In addition, if you have children and you get them involved in your plan, you are effectively helping them to avoid suffering from hypertension in their later lives.

If you already have hypertension it is not too late to start your plan. All of the suggestions in this chapter may help to lower your blood pressure and, in addition, to keep your heart and blood vessels healthy.

Don't forget, your GP is there to help. Most GPs will be delighted if you let them know that you want to do something to tackle hypertension, so ask them for advice!

Help List

Blood Pressure Association

60 Cranmer Terrace, London, SW17 0QS
Tel: 0845 241 0989 (helpline, Monday to Friday, 11am to 3pm)
www.bpassoc.org.uk
A UK-wide charity aiming to lower the nation's blood pressure by providing information, support and awareness raising activities.

British Hypertension Society

www.bhsoc.org
Provides a medical and scientific research forum to understand blood pressure and improve its treatment.

Complementary and Natural Healthcare Council (CNHC)

83 Victoria Street, London, SW1H 0HW
Tel: 0203 178 2199
info@cnhc.org.uk
www.cnhc.org.uk
CNHC operate a voluntary register for practitioners. There is a searchable database on the website.

Dietary Approaches to Stop Hypertension (DASH)

www.dashdiet.org
The DASH diet has been proven to help people lower their blood pressure. The website contains diet tips and recipes and the official recipe book can be purchased through the website.

General Hypnotherapy Register

PO Box 204, Lymington, SO41 6WP
admin@general-hypnotherapy-register.com
www.general-hypnotherapy-register.com
For information on hypnotherapy and a list of practitioners.

High Blood Pressure Foundation

Department of Medical Sciences, Western General Hospital, Edinburgh, EH4 2XU
Tel: 0131 332 9211
hbpf@hbpf.org.uk
www.hbpf.org.uk
A charity dedicated to improve understanding, assessment, treatment and public awareness of high blood pressure.

Keep Fit Association (KFA)

Tel: 01403 266000
kfa@emdp.org
www.keepfit.org.uk
Brings people in similar areas together to exercise.

Patient UK

www.patient.co.uk
For general advice on health and medical conditions. Use the search box to find advice on healthy eating and weight loss.

Smoke Free

Tel: 0800 022 4 332 (helpline, Monday to Sunday, 7am to 11pm)
www.smokefree.nhs.uk
For advice and support on stopping smoking; the website also provides a facility to email an expert for help.

Walking for Health (WFH)

Natural England, John Dower House, Crescent Place, Cheltenham, GL50 3RA
Tel: 0300 060 2287
wfhinfo@naturalengland.org.uk
www.whi.org.uk
Natural England's WFH encourages you to enjoy your local natural spaces and benefit your health by taking part in walks.

Your GP Surgery

Your local GP and practice nurse will be very happy to give you advice or point you in the direction of a local support group for any of the issues covered in this book.

Glossary

Addison's disease
Associated with low blood pressure, a condition where the adrenal glands don't produce enough of the hormones that normally keep your blood pressure up.

Ambulatory blood pressure monitoring
The term used for 24-hour blood pressure monitoring.

Angina pectoris
Angina pectoris (abbreviated to 'angina') is the name given to the pain in the chest caused by a lack of oxygen getting to the heart muscle.

Antihypertensive
The name for medications used to treat high blood pressure.

Aorta
The main blood vessel that carries blood from the heart to the rest of the body.

Artery
Blood vessels that carry blood away from the heart to the rest of the body. All arteries except the pulmonary artery carry oxygenated blood.

Brachial artery
The major blood vessel in the upper arm, this is where the blood pressure monitor is placed in order to measure the blood pressure.

Cardiovascular risk
The risk that you may suffer from a heart attack, angina or stroke. High blood pressure is a contributor to this risk.

Coarctation of the aorta
A condition people are born with which causes the narrowing of the aorta. This, in turn, causes high blood pressure.

Conn's syndrome

Also called hyperaldosteronism – this means that your body is producing too much of the hormone aldosterone. Too much aldosterone causes a high sodium level which, in turn, leads to high blood pressure.

Cushing's syndrome

A condition caused by long term steroid use, symptoms include high blood pressure, weight gain, a hump at the top of the neck, excess hair growth and stretch marks.

Diastolic

This is the lower number of your blood pressure reading. It is the measurement of the residual pressure in the arteries when the heart is relaxed in between beats.

Diuretics

Medication that causes water loss and dehydration. Diuretics help your kidneys to excrete sodium into your urine. The loss of salt and water from your blood stream lowers your blood pressure.

Essential hypertension

Where there is no underlying cause to the high blood pressure, it is a disease in its own right. Also known as primary hypertension.

Gestational hypertension

This develops after 20 weeks of pregnancy and goes away after delivery. In gestational hypertension, pregnancy is the cause of the high blood pressure. However, women who suffer from gestational hypertension are more likely to have high blood pressure later in life.

High normal blood pressure

This is a blood pressure between $^{130}/_{85}$ and $^{139}/_{89}$, also referred to as pre-hypertension.

Hyperaldosteronism

Also called Conn's syndrome – this means that your body is producing too much of the hormone aldosterone. Too much aldosterone causes a high sodium level which, in turn, leads to high blood pressure.

Hyperparathyroidism

In this condition the parathyroid glands are over active, which results in too much calcium in the blood stream. Calcium is similar to sodium in that it increases blood pressure.

Hypertension

The medical description for high blood pressure.

Hypotension

The medical description for low blood pressure.

Isolated diastolic hypertension

When the lower number of your blood pressure is elevated, but the higher number (systolic) is normal.

Isolated systolic hypertension

When the higher number of your blood pressure is elevated, but the lower number (diastolic) is normal.

Malignant hypertension

A rare form of very high blood pressure.

Metabolic syndrome

A combination of hypertension, high cholesterol, diabetes and being overweight. Also known as syndrome X.

Mild hypertension

A blood pressure between $^{140}/_{90}$ and $^{159}/_{99}$.

mmHG

This stands for millimetres of mercury and is the standard way of talking about pressure.

Moderate hypertension

A blood pressure between $^{160}/_{100}$ and $^{180}/_{110}$.

NSAIDS

A type of pain-killer that causes high blood pressure. It stands for non-steroidal anti-inflammatory drugs and includes ibuprofen, aspirin and Voltarol.

Phaeochromocytoma

A growth in the adrenal glands that produces too much of the hormones called adrenalin or noradrenalin. They increase your blood pressure and heart rate and can also make you feel anxious or agitated.

Post prandial hypotension

Low blood pressure after eating. It is more common in people who have high blood pressure and people who are on medications for blood pressure.

Postural hypotension

A sudden fall in blood pressure when a person stands up. Most common amongst people over 65 who are prone to low blood pressure.

Pre-eclampsia

This is a combination of high blood pressure and protein in the urine found after 20 weeks of pregnancy. Pre-eclampsia can be mild, moderate or severe.

Pre-hypertension

This is a blood pressure between $^{130}/_{85}$ and $^{139}/_{89}$, also referred to as high normal blood pressure.

Primary hypertension

Where there is no underlying cause to the high blood pressure and it is a disease in its own right. Also called essential hypertension.

Pulmonary artery

Pulmonary arteries carry blood that is low in oxygen from the heart to the lungs, where it is oxygenated. It is the only artery that carries deoxygenated blood.

Pulmonary vein

The pulmonary vein is the only vein to carry oxygenated blood. It brings it from the lungs back to the heart to be pumped around the rest of the body.

Renal failure

When the kidneys are not functioning properly it is referred to as renal failure or kidney failure.

Renovascular hypertension

In this condition the blood vessels supplying one or both of your kidneys become narrowed meaning that not enough blood gets through to your kidneys. Their response to this is to try to increase the blood pressure so that more blood flows to them.

Secondary hypertension
This is where hypertension is caused by an underlying condition.

Severe hypertension
A blood pressure above $^{180}/_{110}$ is considered as severe hypertension.

Sphygmomanometer
The device used to measure blood pressure.

Syndrome X
A combination of hypertension, high cholesterol, diabetes and being overweight. Also known as metabolic syndrome.

Systolic
This is the upper number of your blood pressure reading. This is the measurement of the pressure caused by the pumping of the heart.

Vein
Veins take deoxygenated blood from the main arteries back to the heart.

White coat hypertension
This is where a blood pressure level will appear elevated due to the stress and anxiety of visiting your GP in a clinical setting.

Need - 2 - Know

Available Titles Include ...

Allergies A Parent's Guide
ISBN 978-1-86144-064-8 £8.99

Autism A Parent's Guide
ISBN 978-1-86144-069-3 £8.99

Drugs A Parent's Guide
ISBN 978-1-86144-043-3 £8.99

Dyslexia and Other Learning Difficulties
A Parent's Guide ISBN 978-1-86144-042-6 £8.99

Bullying A Parent's Guide
ISBN 978-1-86144-044-0 £8.99

Epilepsy The Essential Guide
ISBN 978-1-86144-063-1 £8.99

Teenage Pregnancy The Essential Guide
ISBN 978-1-86144-046-4 £8.99

Gap Years The Essential Guide
ISBN 978-1-86144-079-2 £8.99

How to Pass Exams A Parent's Guide
ISBN 978-1-86144-047-1 £8.99

Child Obesity A Parent's Guide
ISBN 978-1-86144-049-5 £8.99

Applying to University The Essential Guide
ISBN 978-1-86144-052-5 £8.99

ADHD The Essential Guide
ISBN 978-1-86144-060-0 £8.99

Student Cookbook - Healthy Eating The Essential Guide
ISBN 978-1-86144-061-7 £8.99

Stress The Essential Guide
ISBN 978-1-86144-054-9 £8.99

Adoption and Fostering A Parent's Guide
ISBN 978-1-86144-056-3 £8.99

Special Educational Needs A Parent's Guide
ISBN 978-1-86144-057-0 £8.99

The Pill An Essential Guide
ISBN 978-1-86144-058-7 £8.99

University A Survival Guide
ISBN 978-1-86144-072-3 £8.99

Diabetes The Essential Guide
ISBN 978-1-86144-059-4 £8.99

View the full range at **www.need2knowbooks.co.uk**. To order our titles, call **01733 898103**, email **sales@n2kbooks.com** or visit the website.

Need - 2 - Know, Remus House, Coltsfoot Drive, Peterborough, PE2 9JX